Praise for *Obstacles in the Established Church*

"Sam Rainer's book nails it! It is possible to overcome obstacles like resistance to change or high unreasonable expectations and set a new trajectory towards health and growth in an established church. When a pastor provides strong dynamic spiritual leadership that is immersed with love for the people of God, it is possible!

Get this book. Read it. Practice it. Change is on the way!"

Ronnie Floyd
Senior Pastor, Cross Church

"Church planting resources are everywhere nowadays, sometimes leaving pastors in established churches to wonder if anyone understands the unique challenges they face as they lead their congregations. This book answers common questions about common obstacles faced in established churches. Sam Rainer writes with the passion and wisdom he has learned in the trenches of pastoral ministry. Read, lead, and be encouraged."

Trevin Wax
Managing Editor of *The Gospel Project*
Author of *Gospel-Centered Teaching*, *Clear Winter Nights*, *Counterfeit Gospels*, and *Holy Subversion*

"It is no secret that many pastors struggle with leading stagnant, seemingly dying churches. Some, in fact, have given up. Sam Rainer is not one of those pastors. He still believes in the potential of the church because he knows the church is still God's church. This book addresses reality in struggling churches, but it does so with faith and wisdom. It offers proven ideas for pressing forward with hope, balance, and direction. Indeed, the chapter on change is alone worth buying this book. Read it, and take the first steps toward renewal in your church."

Chuck Lawless
Dean of Graduate Studies, Southeastern Baptist Theological Seminary

"This book is full of wisdom, insight, and common sense that too many ministers often miss or forget to their personal harm. Young pastors, in particular, will benefit from this work by Sam Rainer. It may even save your ministry."

Daniel L. Akin
President, Southeastern Baptist Theological Seminary

"Paul gives a great doxology in Romans 16:25 where He prays that the church would be established through the preaching of the gospel. As a church planter who seeks to see young churches become established according to the gospel, I applaud leaders who take on the great and needed ministry of transitioning established churches to greater effectiveness. Pastors will hopefully find in this work the needed tools to strengthen their resolve to see Christ's bride established by the word of God vs human tradition."

Eric Mason
Lead Pastor, Epiphany Fellowship

"Established churches have great opportunities to serve their communities well. They are already known in the community and typically have resources and people. A healthy, established church makes a big and beautiful impact. Leading in an established church presents a unique set of challenges and opportunities, and Sam Rainer offers great insight into both in this book."

Eric Geiger
Vice President, LifeWay Christian Resources

"Pastors of established churches around the world routinely face the frustration that comes with resistance to their leadership. The difficulties of transitioning a church to a healthier course of action in order to reach the world with the gospel are legion. 'Why doesn't this church share my passion for the lost?' 'Why is my church so opposed to a few simple changes that will strengthen our family of faith in so many ways?' In this book, Sam Rainer tackles issues that every pastor has faced at some point in their ministry. This book will not only encourage you to think through the typical obstacles of church leadership practically, it will challenge you to respond to those obstacles biblically while also encouraging you to persevere in your calling. As the pastor of an established church, I give this book my strongest endorsement and encourage you to read it."

Chris Bonts
Senior Pastor, Homesteads Baptist Church, Crossville, Tennessee

Obstacles in the Established Church

How Leaders Overcome Them

Sam S. Rainer III

Obstacles in the Established Church

How Leaders Overcome Them

Sam S. Rainer III

Published by Rainer Publishing
www.rainerpublishing.com

ISBN 978-0692289853

Portions of this book were adapted from SamRainer.com and *Eating the Elephant: Leading the Established Church to Growth* by Thom S. Rainer and Chuck Lawless. © Copyright 2003, Pinnacle Publishers, Louisville, Kentucky.

Unless otherwise noted, all Scripture quotations are taken from the *Holman Christian Standard Bible* (HCSB). Copyright © 1999, 2000, 2002, 2003, 2009 by Holman Bible Publishers. Used by permission.

To Erin, my wife.

To Maggie and Bren, my two daughters.

You bring so much joy in my life.

Throw in Lucy, our dog, and it's one wild home this man wouldn't trade for the world.

Contents

Lights in the Darkness

The obituaries are premature. Yes, I know many churches in North America are dying. Many others are very ill. Indeed, nearly nine out of ten churches in the United States are either declining, or they are growing at a pace that is slower than the community where they are located. In other words, the vast majority of churches are losing ground.

Still, the obituaries are likely premature.

Most had written the obituary of my first church long before I got there. Six people remained at the rural Kentucky congregation. They could not remember the last service.

"I think it was over two years ago," the lone deacon told me. He had more tattoos than teeth, smoked during the service, and occasionally used four-letter words you don't find in the Bible.

But he loved Jesus. So I knew there was hope for the church.

I'll never forget my first Sunday there. I brought my girlfriend (soon to be fiancé). She was the reason we found the church. A pull-tab paper advertisement at her college asked for a preacher. No one had yet pulled any of the tabs. She thought it was the right opportunity for me. She pulled the first tab. I called the number. Herbie, the tattooed, toothless deacon answered. He asked when I thought we should start the service. I thought it was an odd question. So we settled on the next Sunday at 11:00 a.m.

Six people came to worship that Sunday. I have no idea what I preached, but I do remember them talking about the last capital project. The outhouse had been removed a few years prior, and they showed me the new throne room. They were proud. I was grateful.

It was early 2005. And I began bi-vocational ministry at my megachurch of six people. Any pastor worth much at all has lots of "first church" stories. As unhealthy as those first churches can be, and as unhealthy as first-time pastors can be, God does not give up on these congregations. Despite the obvious obstacles, we should not give up on them either.

Some of these churches are beginning to see light in the darkness of decline and despair. They are beginning to have hope. All is not lost.

This book is meant to bring hope for leaders of established churches, leaders who may be frustrated and hurt. Many of you leaders went to your church with great hope for its possibilities, but you quickly encountered resistance and opposition. You found yourself in a position where you either had to engage the opposition or settle for mediocrity with passivity. That hope you once had has now degenerated into pain and skepticism.

You may have been in your church for 15 years (or more) and seen little or no growth. You may have recently come to your church with high expectations, only to be disillusioned in a matter of months. Lack of vitality, petty quarrels, a steady of stream of criticisms, and weak followership may have made you doubt your call to this church or perhaps even to ministry.

Perhaps you now hear the voice of God. You are ready and excited about leading your established church to health and growth.

The good news is that your church can become healthy; it can make a difference. If you are committed to stay, to love your people, and to seek God's face, miracles can happen. Now, we cannot know God's timing, nor can we dictate to Him what must take place in our church. Your church may not soon be on the cover of a magazine that tells the story of its remarkable turnaround, but it can be just as important in God's plan.

In this book, I look at some of the most common obstacles faced by leaders of established churches. I love the established church. I am the pastor of an established church, and I have served as the pastor of other established churches in several regions of the United States. I am writing the dissertation for my Ph.D. in leadership studies, focusing much of my work on the established church. While some of this book represents my own experience, much of it reflects the best of Christian research over the past few years.

Your leadership experiences are unique, as are mine. Your first church might have been larger than mine (few are smaller). Your lone deacon might not have used salty language and smoked in the church during the worship service. While every church is a unique congregation in a specific local context, I have found that patterns present in one established church are typically present in another. I have identified many of those patterns, particularly the obstacles that often hinder these churches toward health and growth. I will identify the major obstacles and address how many church leaders have successfully overcome them.

This book is intentionally brief. It's not meant to be an exhaustive study on every obstacle in the established church. I hope you can read it in a couple of sittings. The conclusions—though based on research—are not meant to be scientific findings. I write this book not as a scientific study but rather as realistic way to encourage many of you grinding your way through ministry at established churches. As a leader in a church facing many obstacles, you may feel like you are the only light shining brightly. But you're not. You may feel like you're burning out. But there's hope. You may feel like the obstacles are too much. They are not. The gates of hell cannot stand against God's church. It's time we get on the offensive. It's time we charge. It's time we faced these obstacles and led our congregations through them.

Many years ago, I read an interview with Billy Graham. The interviewer seemed to be curious about the evangelist's opinion of his own ministry. The interviewer asked if Graham anticipated being given great rewards in heaven for the millions of lives he had impacted though his worldwide ministry. Billy Graham responded that he was not certain of the extent of his own rewards, but it was certain that others would have greater rewards than he. He said that somewhere in the world today, a faithful elderly woman is on her knees praying for her little country church, her family, and her pastor. Billy Graham could imagine that, for 80 years the sweet lady has been faithful to her Lord. She has prayed, read the Bible daily, and taught children in Sunday school. To the evangelist, that lady and scores like her will receive the greatest rewards in heaven. The closing words of the interview will be forever etched in my memory: "You see," said Graham, "we are not called to be successful. We are called to be faithful."

It is my prayer that this book will rekindle the fire in your heart, a desire for nothing less than total faithfulness to our Lord. And that new desire will result in a renewed, confident passion to lead your established church, to love even when some members are unlovable. In the midst of this rekindled desire, you will see God work through you to overcome the obstacles that have hindered your ministry to this point.

It is my prayer that this book will indeed rekindle that desire of faithfulness and godly leadership. If you are ready for this journey, will you join me in the following prayer?

Dear Lord, I confess that I have not always been the leader of the church that you have called me to be. Selfish motives and hurt feelings have sometimes surpassed my desires to be faithful to you. And sometimes fears of failures and criticism have paralyzed me. I repent of these sins.

Now I am ready, excited, and willing to lead Your church. I wait on You and Your timing. I will let you define success for me. And free me from unhealthy and ungodly comparisons and competition.

Use me Lord to lead Your church to health and growth. Help me to love Your children in this church unconditionally. Remind me that, even though I am a serial sinner, You went to the cross and died for me. You loved me unconditionally. And so should I love those in this church. And when difficulties arise, remind me to keep my eyes on You.

Thank you in advance for Your victories in Your church. I anticipate the great work You will do in the days ahead. To God be the glory! In Jesus' name. Amen.

Now, let's take a look at each of those major obstacles. There are none that will surprise you. But let's see how God can use you to get beyond them to the point of victory after victory. Let's see what you can do in His power to overcome the obstacles in the established church. To those challenges and victories we now turn.

Chapter 2

Change

"We've Never Done It That Way Before!"

You have probably heard about this church. Its story has been in print for quite a while. The church was new, assembling together after the departure of their leader. From a human perspective, their future was bleak. No one outside the church expected them to succeed. Probably some of the church members themselves were wavering in their faith as well, but they tenaciously held to their conviction that something great was about to happen. Well something did happen. Something almost unbelievable happened.

This church exploded. From a faithful few, three thousand became followers of Christ and were baptized *in one day!* And the growth and conversions continued daily. The church, of course, was the first church. The town was Jerusalem. And the story of the explosive growth is detailed in Acts 1-7.

Now you might expect that such a church would not have to deal with some of the same issues as those in the established church. Such unparalleled evangelistic growth may seem to have little in common with the many struggling established churches today. But all churches, to different degrees, are confronted with the not-always-so-pleasant constant called change.

I suspect that the first church handled the initial change well. After all, the words of Jesus' promise had been fulfilled at Pentecost. The power of the Holy Spirit was on the church. Thousands were following Christ. The people of Jerusalem were in awe of the church. Excitement abounded. Hope was fulfilled. The rag-tag followers of Christ were making an obvious difference in the Kingdom. This type of change was obviously well received.

But another major change impacted the church later. Jesus had commissioned the church to be witnesses not only in Jerusalem, but "in all Judea and Samaria, and to the ends of the earth" as well (Acts1:8). The church responded obediently to the first part of the command; the followers were definitely witnesses in Jerusalem. But what happened to the obedience to the other parts of the command—to extend the witness to all of Judea,

Samaria, even to the ends of the earth? Is it possible that the church was satisfied with its work? Was there resistance in responding to leave Jerusalem? Did the change associated with leaving their homes just seem too painful?

Whatever their motives for remaining in Jerusalem, the church did not initially fulfill all of Christ's command. God eventually allowed persecution of the church so that the people would scatter (Acts 8:4). Men, women, and children left their homes and moved to other locations to escape persecution. The gospel was proclaimed wherever these believers traveled. Is it possible that such fierce persecution was necessary to initiate change in the early church? Was this action necessary to break the holy huddles in Jerusalem?

While some of the points are speculative, the central theme is the same: Churches have been dealing with change since Pentecost. One of the most important factors in the health of a church is the manner in which its leaders initiate and handle change. It is especially critical in the established church.

Resistance to Change

Almost everyone has a part of them that does not like change. Big changes do not bother me, but small changes trouble my soul. Moving to a new city is not a problem for me. That's a big change. But the small change of rearranging my wardrobe, now that messes with my head. My wife recently came to me with a tattered pair of boxers.

"It's time to let them go," she said.

"But they're comfortable."

"No, they're shredded."

"I've had them since high school. See the initials on the tag? My mom put them there with a sharpie so my clothes wouldn't get mixed up with my brother's clothes."

"You're 33," she said.

"But I like being able to tell the students at church I have underwear older than them."

I do not like change. Neither do most of the people in your church. That tattered hymnal, that lumpy pew cushion, that dusty electric organ—people can hang on to them like an old pair of boxers. It doesn't make much sense, other than change is difficult, even small change.

I should have remembered this principle when I tried to lead a previous church to switch worship times. The traditional service would move to the 8:30 a.m. slot, and the contemporary service would take the 11:00 a.m. time. It was a simple change, nothing fundamental. Everyone could still have their service just the way they like, albeit at a different time. The resistance and opposition were fierce. The pain was real. The tension was palpable. I received hate mail. Two deacons bordered on needing an exorcism. I promise I saw their heads spin around.

I backed down.

When we lead established churches to change, we must respect and understand the feelings of those who resist change. Yet at the same time, if the issue is truly one of eternal importance, we must press on. "We've never done it that way before" is often cited as the seven last words of a dying church. A close relative to that statement is "We've tried it before, but it didn't work." These statements alone are not the true obstacles to change, but they do point to four hurdles.

Four Hurdles to Change

Does the established nature of some churches hinder innovation? Is an established structure antithetical to quick, nimble changes? For most established churches, yes, but it does not mean established churches cannot innovate or change.

A church plant is an innovation. I define innovation as the process of successfully establishing something new. To introduce something new—and to get it to work longer than a month—is innovation. Perhaps some luck into the right change at the right time. Perhaps some churches land on the right demographic with the right leadership. Not all innovations are intentional or well-planned. But an effective church plant should be noted as innovation.

As churches become more established, they tend to be less prone to change. By its nature, an established church has a system in place that pushes against change. To establish is to create firm stability. Churches need stability. For example, a discipleship process that is not rooted into the culture of the church (or established) is not likely to last long. And it's only a matter of time before the innovative church plant begins to feel the pull of becoming established. Everything is new only once, after all.

While stability is necessary, every church should also innovate. Established churches, in particular, can take comfort in the establishment. Traditions and history can easily become a guise for complacency. Change can take a back seat to the entrenched processes that help create the stability. So what hurdles to change exist in the established church? Here are four examples.

The first hurdle is a *lack of intentionality*. Generally, established churches have more resources than new churches. When resources are limited, churches must be more intentional about innovation. Failure—especially one that is expensive—can quickly derail a church with limited resources. When resources are plentiful, the temptation is to be less intentional. Established churches can generally absorb more failures. But a practice of spaghetti-against-the-wall-and-see-what-sticks is not true innovation. It's haphazard chaos. Give it a month and see how many people get annoyed.

The second hurdle is a *lack of originality*. Established churches should build on their foundations, but please don't slap a new logo on an existing program and call it innovation. Innovation is introducing something new, not introducing something with the façade of newness.

The third hurdle is the *wrong metrics*. What gets measured gets done, and what you measure is typically an indicator of what you value. A mature church will measure different things than a new church. Most church plants are not attempting to track down meeting minutes from a dozen committees for next week's business meeting. And established churches don't have to worry about the retention ratio of people from a launch service. However, an overemphasis on the metrics sustaining the establishment will inevitably deemphasize innovation and dissuade team members from attempting change.

The fourth hurdle is the *ease of appeasement*. In an established church some leaders prefer the ease of appeasing members rather than changing to reach new people. Obviously, a long-term member may not desire to be appeased, but rather challenged. However, most churches have a segment of people who would rather rest in the stability of the establishment. It's not necessarily a sin issue, and leaders should care about all members whatever their spiritual maturity. Appeasing existing members, however, is much easier than challenging a church to change and reach new people. Even in a healthy established church—one ready to reach outwardly—change is a challenge. The typical established church has several groups of people who joined during different seasons of the church for different reasons. Even when people agree to reach outwardly, getting them to agree on timing, direction, budgeting, and pace is a challenge. It's easier to appease. But appeasement never leads to positive change.

Though established churches are not new, they can still introduce new things. They can innovate. They can change. Hurdles exist. These hurdles, however, are surmountable. Later in this chapter, I'll share some principles to help guide you through the change process. Before I get to *what* churches must do to change, let's examine *why* people resist change.

Why Your Church Resists the Concept of Change

"It's my first week, what should I change here?" Perhaps new pastors don't vocalize the question, but I know they think it. The default setting to change something is only natural for a good leader. Having a vision means being dissatisfied with the status quo.

"The search committee said they were bringing me on to make needed changes. Why is the church resisting the obvious?!" Why have so many pastors' honeymoons ended after the first month? Resistance to change is one of the largest hurdles in leadership. I once had a handful of pencils launched my way when my tweaks to a potluck dinner were discovered. I learned not to mess with potlucks. Luckily the pencils weren't that sharp, and they no longer contain lead. No blood, no foul. Every church leader has been there. We've all met the resistance. Understanding why your congregation resists change will help you guide them through change.

Let's begin with pastors who are new to a church. The first thing to realize is that you are the change. Even if you change nothing—and I mean absolutely nothing—in your first year as a pastor, then people will still experience a huge change: you. You are not new to yourself, but you certainly are new to the people of the church. Any change efforts you introduce in your first few months are only magnified by the fact that people are still trying to get to know who you are.

A second reason churches resist change has to do with leaders who do not properly recognize the type of change they are recommending. There are *technical* changes and *cultural* changes, and these two types of change are entirely different. When people say they want change, they often mean technical changes. Technical problems require a specific expertise. For many, pastors are seen as the hired expert on hand to work through technical problems. People desiring technical changes ask these types of questions: Can you make sure my curriculum is in my room? Can you see that the church is not so hot in the summer? Why haven't I received the newsletter? These questions involve small technical changes, but often people desire large technical changes too, like a new building.

Technical changes are important. If you pastor a church of any size, then you must manage the organization of people. Few people, however, understand that lasting change is cultural, not technical. Cultural problems are not solved by just a technical expert, but rather these changes involve a general acceptance of everyone. If you are a leader, then you're most likely gravitating towards the cultural changes you believe need to be made. That's what leaders do. They challenge the status quo. But you must realize that very few people in your church default to cultural changes. There's a reason why some things get imbedded in the culture of a church. Most people find them acceptable.

Let me give you an example of technical and cultural changes. Perhaps this example will hit close to home. At a previous church, the worship pastor and I made an easy technical change. It took about an hour. We set up drums. Then we used the drums in the worship service. Easy change, right? Nope. The post-service conversations still echo today.

"Drums drum up demons!"

"That rock music doesn't belong in church!"

"We're not going to become one of those churches!"

"We should play heaven's music, not Satan's music!"

"Just stick with the organ because it's biblical!"

Every part of me wanted to argue. I wanted to push back. I wanted to show how electricity had not been invented at the time of John the Baptist, so an electric organ could in no way be "biblical." Their attitudes stunk. But my motivation was wrong.

I wanted them to change, but rather than doing the hard work of dealing with the culture in the church, I decided to force-feed technical changes. Most technical changes are relatively easy compared with the harder work of leading cultural change. The reason some in the church pushed back against drums is not because they opposed the instrument *technically*. We used CD tracks with the choir that contained drums. For my detractors, putting them in the church was a symbol to them that went against the *culture* of the congregation. They associated drums with the rebellion of the 1960s' rock music movement. And they did not want rebellion represented in the church. Rather than methodically teaching people about the importance of contextualizing the music in worship, I simply made a technical change. And of course, the change did not stick within the culture.

A third reason churches resist change has to do with the one proposing the change (which is most likely you). Just because people like you and send nice cards doesn't necessarily mean they fully trust you. Even when people respect the office of pastor, not knowing the person who fills that spot often leads to a cautious acceptance from the congregation. Respect and trust are two different mindsets. People may respect you while not fully trusting you. Earn their trust by honoring their respect before making big moves.

A fourth reason churches resist change is the belief that change is not necessary. It's a key question: Do the people I'm leading even recognize the need for change? If the current way appears successful, then the evidence of a problem is hidden from the plain sight of the people. As the leader, you may have the advantage of inside organizational knowledge. A knowledge to which the average churchgoer may have zero exposure. Before you implement a change effort, you have to show people the hidden problem.

A fifth reason churches resist change is the belief that change is not feasible. Even if everyone agrees that change would be good, not everyone may agree that change is feasible. It's easier to show people the problem than it is the feasibility of fixing the problem. Getting people to agree on a common problem is not enough. To enact lasting change, you must also show them how the solution is feasible.

Lastly, people will resist a change effort if it reshuffles the power alignment. Rare is the breed of person who willingly gives up position, status, or power without some resistance. This resistance makes sense. If someone challenged your position, then you would likely resist that effort as well. Though most people are rightly repulsed by the idea of the church being a political organization, forming political allies is a necessity in every organization. Before you challenge the current power structure of a church, serve and befriend the power brokers. If you can win them over, then you will have their help in enacting long-term cultural changes.

Remember, people react emotionally when you challenge their values and ideals. When change is viewed as an assault on a current set of ideals and values, you can expect widespread resistance. These values may not be what's formally published in the constitution and bylaws. The only way to uncover these values and ideals is to spend time with different people. Detached pastors will never know the unspoken—yet well understood—values of their congregants.

Change is likely to occur when the people within an organization believe the benefits of making the change outweigh the costs of making the change. And this attitudinal shift doesn't come easily or quickly!

Why Your Church Resists the Implementation of Change

If you lead well, then resistance to change will eventually shift to an acceptance of the necessity of change. Even when people accept the concept of change, however, the actual implementation of the change effort can be painful. For example, most Americans agree something needs to change at the IRS. I doubt we'll see many lawmakers defend the current state of the agency on cable news stations. Does this general acceptance mean enduring change will now happen quickly? I have my doubts.

Church leaders often encounter a strong contingent within their congregations who accept the need for change, even the enduring cultural change I mentioned in the previous section. The size of this group depends upon the church, but they are inevitably there. As your tenure lengthens, this group should grow as more people begin to trust your discernment. Conversely, if this group is shrinking, then stop reading and start building better relationships. Leading change while your reputation diminishes is a suicide mission. Assuming you have done the legwork to get most people accepting the need for change, why might this change effort still meet resistance as you implement it?

First, most organizations are too complex for one person to lead a change effort. The median church size is approximately 75 people. Any organization of 75—church or not—is a complex system of relationships, opinions, maturity (or immaturity), and attitudes. Is it feasible that one person can lead a change effort at the IRS? No way. And it's just as unfeasible that you alone are going to be the cause and effect at your church. Lone rangers are just that—they work alone. And you don't wear a mask. Your church knows where you live. Enduring cultural change only happens if it is *led* (not just accepted) by a coalition of those with positional power, expertise, experience, and credibility. In short, if key members are not on board, then it's unlikely your change effort lasts in the culture of the church.

Second, change efforts come with a cost. While we often refer to the cliché synergy of change efforts, the reality is many changes are zero-sum: You must sacrifice one area to gain in another area. For example, if you change a church to be more flexible, then it often leads to a decrease in efficiency. Flexibility adds options, and more options mean more decisions, which reduces efficiency. For instance, if you allow for multiple types of small groups in your church (i.e. open and closed), then you are more flexible. However, managing multiple types of small groups takes more time and is less efficient. Enduring cultural change occurs when a coalition of leaders agree on what is to be sacrificed in order to enact the change.

Third, the pace of change is just as important as the change itself. Do you create a crisis to ramrod sudden change? If so, then you must be willing to intimidate and act forcibly. Do you allow for gradualism? Some changes can happen over time, but these changes may also slowly evolve in a way unintended. Let me give you a few examples to help answer these questions.

Move quickly through change with doctrine and discipline issues. These issues have little middle ground. A person either believes in a specific doctrine or not. A person is either repentant or not. For example, you should not slowly remove a group leader if she outright denies a primary tenet of the church. Such change must happen quickly.

Move slowly through change in stages with structural, staff, and non-biblical issues. It's unwise (if not sheer stupidity) to restructure the staff in your first month before you even have a grasp everyone's job descriptions and callings. Learn the current system—and more importantly the people within the system—before radicalizing it.

Move slowly through change if it's your first church. You may be right about many things that need to change, but you are likely wrong about how to change them. If you don't think you need leadership experience to change a church, then you need more experience. Don't learn the hard way.

Change is not the most important role for church leaders. Don't attempt change if you haven't learned to love the people of the church *and* the community. If you haven't had supper with a dozen members, you're not ready to lead change. If you don't know the name of the deacon chairman's spouse, you're not ready to lead change. If you can't succinctly describe your group structure, you're not ready to lead change. You cannot lead a church forward unless you love your church where it is now, not where you hope it will be in the future. Change is important. But true change does not happen without love.

Making Your Ideas Work for You, Not Against You

In 1948 two graduate students at the Drexel Institute of Technology overheard a supermarket executive discussing a key problem: the need for an automatic system to read each product item. Working together, the two students helped change the way retailers do business. They came up with this idea called a bar code.

Before the bar code, supermarket clerks had to punch numbers into a keypad. It was slow. The process was prone to keystroke errors. After the bar code, everything scanned swiftly and with minimal errors (and thank goodness for the self check-out lanes—impossible without the bar code).

We experience the change to the bar code system almost every day. It's ubiquitous. But how did the idea transition to reality? What can churches learn from this process?

Ideas that transition into long-term changes are typically simple and have obvious benefits. How many times have I said, "Why didn't I think of that?" The best ideas are simple. The best ideas have obvious benefits. The bar code was simple—just a bunch of lines inspired by the dots and dashes of Morse code. And yet the benefits were profound.

Are you floating simple ideas or complex ideas to your leaders? Are the benefits obvious? Not every idea needs to be simple. Indeed many changes in the church are complex, involving a cultural shift among the people. But the ones most quickly adopted are simple with obvious benefits.

Additionally, change lasts longest when it involves a standard process. The great Wally World of Bentonville gave the bar code a boost. As Wal-Mart grew (along with other large grocery chains), so did the use of the rather efficient bar code, which became a critical part of retail distribution systems. Critical mass was achieved, however, with the adoption of a standard system. The scanners were expensive to retailers. Manufacturers had to change systems to put the labels on all the products. Without a standard bar code, each retailer would have its own system and each manufacturer its own label. When the National Association of Food Chains chose the UPC bar code as the standard, enough companies jumped on board to make it a reality.

If you're mulling through an idea that will be a different reality for different groups in the church, then you're less likely to see the idea transition into change. If the change effort is not standard for the entire church, then people are likely to be confused. For instance, having two discipleship processes for two groups is likely to produce misunderstandings and misperceptions. The more a leader can make a new idea relevant to the entire church, the likelier that idea will transition into change.

The bar code went through several phases. The original design was a circle. But designers soon discovered during printing that the ink would smudge in the direction of the running paper. So the linear form we know today was created. The original creators of the circular bar code could have scoffed at the proposed change, but they were flexible. The idea was not about shape or form but rather use.

If you're working through an idea for your church, then make it simple, standard, and... flexible. Neither simplicity nor standards should become so rigid that—as the change implementation begins—an idea cannot evolve over time. A good idea becomes better through the multi-workings of the people in the church. As the leader, most changes will begin with your ideas. But your ideas are not the endpoint. The best vision for an established church combines the simplicity of a leader's idea with the involvement of the people. As a leader, you must be flexible with your ideas in order for the entire congregation to make them their own.

It's fun to dream up new ideas. The hard work begins in attempting to implement new ideas. Change occurs most smoothly when ideas are simple, standard, and flexible. So, what are some principles to help guide you along the change process? The next section details a few of these principles.

Principles for Change

There has been much written about change, but there is still much to learn. And many of the so-called experts of change management don't really help when we apply their principles to our situations in the church. Despite the challenges, though, we can influence change. We can be proactive. Indeed it is possible for us to be successful.

If understanding change is important for all leaders, it is critically important for leaders of established churches. I would imagine that most American churches today fit the descriptions of the "more resistant" categories. In other words, change can be very difficult in an established church. Understanding some of the basic tenets about change will help the established church pastor over many potential hurdles.

1. Begin with Prayer

A consistent facet of my prayer life is the prayer for wisdom. "If any of you lacks wisdom, he should ask God, who gives to all generously and without criticizing, and it will be given to him" (James1:5). God-given discernment for a change agent is a requisite. Tough decisions must be made. The promise from God's Word is that He will give us the wisdom in all decisions. The value of all the leadership books and courses in the world pales in comparison to the value of this one promise.

A praying pastor is obvious to church members. The pastor is dependent on God and demonstrates a humility that comes with that dependence. His desire for change is not that he will have his way, but that God's will be done. Resistant people can become receptive people through the power of prayer. If mountains can be moved through faith and prayer, then established churches can become open to change through prayer.

2. Love the People

The higher the level of trust of the pastor by the people, the more receptive church members will be to change. While several factors influence the level of trust, none is greater than the pastor's love of the people. Such love cannot be contrived; it must be genuine. A commitment must be made by the pastor that he will love the members of his church unconditionally.

It does not take long for that love to be tested. Cantankerous and critical members will try the patience of the most loving of pastors. How he responds to these people will be both a test of love and of credibility. While he may disagree strongly with a member, his response can be couched in prayerful love.

3. Choose Your Battles

I recently read an analysis of a politician's rapid decline in support and popularity. His reelection chances were slim because of his unwillingness to compromise. He insisted on having his way on almost every issue.

Leaders of established churches must realize that many issues are simply not worth fighting over. If our church members see in us a flexibility and willingness to compromise on minor and non-essential issues, they are more likely to support us on major issues. Of course, any issue that threatens doctrinal integrity cannot be compromised, but the great majority of battles in established churches are not theological in nature.

4. Realize Your Own Imperfections

My father told the story to my brothers and me about what he called one of his dumb mistakes in ministry. At a monthly church business meeting, the church staff presented a proposal to increase the budget by $30,000 for some unplanned equipment needs. The questions and suggestions continued for almost an hour until our dad stood up and said, "Folks, you called me to be the leader of this church. I wish you would end this discussion and trust us to make the right decision."

The problem was that the proposed purchase was not the best price, and many astute businesspersons in the meeting knew better. He had consulted no one. My father told me that his credibility took a nosedive that evening. Several months passed before many key leaders began to trust him again.

One of his biggest steps to regaining credibility was to apologize publicly to the church and to admit his mistakes and imperfections. It was a tough lesson for him. I guess that's why he wanted to remind his sons.

A strong leader seeks the wisdom of others. A change agent realizes that his way may not be the best way. He admits his mistakes and misjudgments. He is willing to compromise on non-essential issues. His personality is truly transparent. His confidence is based on strength in

God; his transparency is the result of his willingness to admit his imperfections.

5. Affirm Traditions

Everyone is a traditionalist to some degree. I take the same route home almost every day. I look forward to seeing my wife and two daughters, and even my dog, at about the same time each day. *Tradition* is not bad. *Traditionalism*, the worship of tradition, is a violation of the first of the Ten Commandments.

We can know that we are practicing traditionalism if our traditions interfere with our obedience to God. Sometimes traditions must be broken to reach people for Christ or to be more effective in ministry, but many traditions can be affirmed and celebrated.

Find those traditions in your church that you can affirm. I served as a pastor of a church that began the missions offering for my denomination. I was able to affirm that century-old tradition again and again. It was a reminder to the members that I was not anti-tradition. Change leadership will go much more smoothly if past, present, and future are seen as an ongoing statement to what God has purposed.

6. Build on Successes

I know a pastor of an established church who made a decision after several years of ministry to begin giving credit to the members of his church for any and all of the church's successes. He further decided that any blame for the lack of victories would be his own. Church members would not be blamed; their perceived inadequacies would be the result of inadequate leadership.

The pastor told me that this decision was life-transforming for him. A whole new realm of accountability was created because "the buck stopped" with him. The elders, deacons, naysayers, or apathetic members would not be blamed. Responsibility would be his and his alone. He would do everything in God's power to achieve God's victories in the church. The pastor was directly accountable to God for the church's failures and successes.

By accepting full leadership responsibility for the church, the pastor soon discovered more effective leadership skills. He learned that often the best timing for a change is soon after a victory or series of victories in the church. Change is often accepted after a leader has demonstrated his ability to lead a church successfully.

7. Allow for Open Discussion

An established church typically has been doing many things the same way for several years. Change can take place, but the pace must be slower than that of an established church. The members need the opportunity to discuss the proposed change in both formal and informal settings. And the discussions in the Monday morning coffee shop may be more important than those in a formal church gathering.

Not only is open communication important, it is also essential that no information be withheld. Every church member should feel that he or she has all the information pertinent to the change. An abundance of relevant information engenders a spirit of openness and trust.

8. Demonstrate Wisdom in Timing

Unlike a church planting situation where

everything is new, the established church typically is not equipped emotionally to handle rapid change. The timing of each change is critical. Often there should be spaces or buffers between changes to allow the congregation to adjust. Leaders in an established church often must have a long-term view. Change just cannot come at the pace most leaders would prefer.

9. Keep the Focus

Up to this point, I have been describing several precautions that the established church pastor should observe in process of initiating change. It should be understood clearly, however, that these precautions are not to be points of distraction. The leader must keep the focus on moving the church toward greater health. While the pace and the frequency of change may be slower and more methodical than the pace in a newer church, the established church must nevertheless make consistent progress in reaching more people for Christ with the gospel, and becoming more effective in ministry.

10. Allow for a Trial Period

Some changes may be made on a trial basis. (Obviously a building program would be an exception). Change-resistant members can be comforted by knowing that the intrusion into their comfort zone may not be permanent. At the end of the trial period, one of three decisions can be made: (1) extend the trial period to allow for further evaluation; (2) reverse the change; or (3) make the change permanent. If the latter choice is made, the benefits of the change will have become obvious to most people. Some members, however, will resist and resent the change regardless of the obvious benefit.

Perhaps you heard the story of the 100-year-old man who was interviewed by a local newspaper reporter. The reporter commented that the old man must have seen a lot of changes in his century of life. The man responded: "Yep, and I didn't like none of 'em!" Some church members will notice the changes and they "won't like none of 'em." That observation brings us to the next point.

11. Expect Opposition

A pastor told me the story of a fascinating exercise he conducted. Everyone who attends a worship service has the opportunity to complete a registration card that is found in the worship folder. The cards serve a multitude of purposes. They provide space for prayer requests, and encourage requests for information. They allow the member or guest the opportunity to communicate an important decision or commitment, such as a desire to become a follower of Christ. Also, they serve as a general communication vehicle, where anyone can make a comment, either positive or negative.

The church is large, so members and guests turn in hundreds of cards each week. The pastor saved all the cards, a few thousand, for a month. He asked his assistant to divide them into several stacks. One of the stacks represented the critical comments noted via this communicate card.

The pastor said he was surprised in two ways. First, the stack of critical comment cards was very small compared to all the cards the church received. Second, most of the criticisms came from a handful of members in the church, hardly representative of the overall positive attitude of most members. Those few critics, though, had noted the changes in the church but "didn't like none of 'em." Some people will never be pleased!

Criticism and opposition can drain a pastor emotionally and spiritually. After a while, the leader may be tempted to refrain from initiating any significant change because of the potential criticism the change may engender. Such an attitude will result in lost opportunities for growth and ministry. The pastor must seek God's wisdom to discern the proper balance between the extremes of being like a bulldozer or a pet rock in initiating change.

Receiving criticism is a fact of life for leaders and especially for pastors who are making genuine efforts to lead established churches to greater health. Expect some level of opposition with any significant decision but love your critics, even the unlovable ones. Show respect for and to them, even though they may treat you disrespectfully. Pray for them. And keep your eyes on Jesus as you stay focused on leading His bride, the church, to greater health.

12. Evaluate Change

Not every change is good. Not every change will work. Evaluate decisions on a regular and systematic basis. Be willing to admit that a particular change did not work. But give a new ministry, program, or idea time to work. Do not concede easily if the change is a deep conviction of yours. The God who gave you the vision will see you through the most difficult of times.

Some of those difficult times include dealing with intense criticisms. But that is the subject of the next chapter. To that issue we now turn.

Chapter 3

Criticism

"I Love You Pastor, But..."

Oliver Adderholt was a good pastor. Not a perfect pastor, but a good pastor. He had been at Golden Road Church for three years. For the most part, the time with the church had been positive. But Oliver lived with the problem most pastors and other leaders face—criticism.

Oliver had learned that criticism comes in different ways and in varying forms and degrees. Rarely is the attack direct, but all of the criticisms hurt. One form of criticism that particularly bothered him was the type that was poorly hidden by a compliment: "Pastor, you know we love you, but. . ." That comment reminded him of lines that he had recently read in a book: "It was a good sermon, pastor, but a little long." That line was not humorous to him. You can be sure that the pastor heard only "but a little long" and carried that around for a few days.

Another form of criticism that was too common to Oliver was the "important-petty" comments. Pastor Adderholt remained amazed at how some church members made such a big deal over small matters. I must admit that I too am amazed at what I hear from some my fellow pastors. "You need a haircut pastor." "You should turn off your microphone when you sing, pastor, because you can't carry a tune." "Why do you wear those clothes, pastor?"

Perhaps the most irksome to Oliver was "People are saying that. . ." He thought it was particularly cowardly for church members to hide behind the comments of others. *Let them tell me to my face if they have a problem with me,* thought Oliver. But on the second thought he really did not want to deal with a truckload of critics.

The critics this time were particularly vociferous. Pastor Adderholt had been actively involved in the selection of a new staff member. Continuity of staff in this particular case was critical. Fortunately, the former staff member had shared confidentially about his potential move a few months before he left. Oliver was able to obtain the resumes and recommendations of several candidates by the time the former staff member left.

When a search committee was formed to look for a new staff member, the pastor shared with the committee the names of several good candidates. He also told them of his prior knowledge of the former staff member's departure, which gave him an opportunity to look for candidates. The committee was very grateful for his work and, as a result, had a candidate to recommend to the church within a few weeks.

That is when the criticisms began. The first came from a particularly negative person who was certain that the selection process was not "by the books." The pastor was flabbergasted by the innuendo. Though the process had been swift, he had been faithful to the rules in spirit and law. *In no way*, he thought, *did he deserve that criticism*.

Then came the long, single-spaced email. The writer had delivered her epistles before, but this one seemed especially harsh and sanctimonious.

The final blow came when Mark, the usual bearer of bad tidings, told Oliver that "people were saying" that the selection process had been railroaded. *Railroaded!* Oliver shouted to himself.

He had done nothing but try to move the church through a possible difficult time. He had anticipated gratitude from the church. None came. Just criticism and more criticism.

Oliver unloaded his emotions that night with his wife. Together they discussed the events of the past three years. There had been many good times, but the criticisms had been ever present. They wondered together if their relatively brief ministry at Golden Road Church should end.

A Strategy for Nastygrams

Like Oliver, we've all received them. If you're a pastor, then you probably know of the nastygram. Every so often someone will send an unwarranted, venomous note, letter, or email. In the church, these malicious messages are usually about irrelevant specifics, not the essentials of discipleship or the direction of a leader's vision. Most annoyingly, they can come as a surprise from someone who has never expressed any previous disagreements in person.

I'll never forget one anonymous note I received on the back of an offering envelope (of all things). It read, "Bring back the poinsettias or else!" Apparently, someone had moved the potted reds during the Christmas season. I had not noticed their new placement, so I inquired with my staff.

"Ah, we moved 'em since Jane has a deathly allergy," my maintenance guy told me.

"She's allergic to poinsettias?"

"Yup, didn't want her to die in the service and all."

"Works for me."

Since the note was anonymous, I had no way of contacting the offended party to tell how the beloved poinsettias were poison, which was why they moved from the stage to another part of the church. I also wondered what "or else" meant, but I assumed it involved some dreaded torture of participating in flannel graph lessons for hours on end. So I dropped the issue. But I did keep the note and placed it in my "Coo-coo for Cocoa Puffs" file, which is where many of the nastygrams go.

Regardless of how off base such a letter may be, it still represents the perspective of a person in the church family. So what do you do? Obviously, leaders do not lead by people-pleasing. And anonymous letters make for good practice at trash can basketball. However, nastygrams from members willing to put their names on them deserve a response. As leaders, we must be intentional in how we deal with everything, especially upset church members. Here are four strategies.

You can ignore them. Sometimes people really are senseless—giving them an audience only worsens the problem. As we will explore more in this chapter, ignoring criticism can be a useful tactic. Some notes (and people) do not deserve a response. Most often, however, ignoring people is generally bad leadership. Pretending problems don't exist is foolish.

You can pout. People-pleasers (most of us leaders) hate to get these types of notes and messages. It brings us down. It consumes our thoughts. We mope. We sulk about as if no one else appreciates us. Pouting gets you nowhere. Pouting can also cause your supporters to think less of you.

You can fight back. This is the worst option—using your leadership skills to trade insults. The temptation is great to fire back a pithy, rancorous email. But such banter does not honor God. Leaders in the church are called to be above reproach, not below the belt.

You can lead. Use the nastygram as an opportunity to reach out to people and enlighten them to the greater purpose of your vision. Put their concern in the grander perspective of where you are headed as a leader. Perhaps they have bad information about you. Perhaps their bitter message is the result of gossip from others. Buried in the insult, perhaps they have a point. You might have the opportunity to build a bridge to an entire group of people. You might gain a stronger ally after graciously reaching out. In every case, you have the opportunity to show the love of Christ.

With all nastygrams, it's important not to focus on them. Don't let them consume you. And I hope your files are like mine. I've received piles (literally) of encouraging notes and letters from people of all generations at my church. The nastygram is a rarity. When it comes, I try to use it as an opportunity. It's tough—and I've not always responded appropriately—but I've never regretted responding by speaking the truth in love.

Pastors in Pain

While the expectations of pastors are high, respect for the position has been declining steadily for years. One of the few consolations a minister has from the ongoing "most respected" polls is that his profession is held in higher esteem than that of politicians!

Numerous theories have been proposed about the declining respect for ministers. One simply says that Christianity has declined in its respect and numbers of adherents; therefore the decline in respect of its leaders is to be expected. Another position holds that the ministry has become more professionalized, resulting in the same expectations for a pastor as one might have for a corporate CEO. Another popular view is the "televangelist theory." Certainly the moral misconduct of many highly visible ministers can explain the problem partially.

In reality several factors probably combine to account for the declining respect of ministers. Pastors are in pain. Perhaps you're feeling this pain right now as you read. Regardless of the explanations, pastors and other staff ministers are confronted daily with a more hostile environment than years past, and much of that hostility is found within the church herself.

Tenure and Criticism

One of the continuing themes in this book is

that patience is needed as God does His work through you in an established church. I remain convinced and convicted that God desires to breathe new life into stale and staid churches. Yet I am also convinced that He waits on pastors who are committed to stay with a church. He will send real revivals when leaders are in place to guide their churches through those revivals.

When we look at God's honor roll in the Bible, we see people committed to their callings and places of service regardless of circumstances. People like Noah (Hebrews 11:7), Abraham (v. 8), Joseph (v. 22), and Moses (v. 24), to name a few, held fast in their callings with patience and courage. And who can doubt the commitment of the apostle Paul? He stayed with God's call despite floggings, beatings, shipwrecks, danger, hunger, thirst, exposure, and imprisonment (2 Corinthians 11:23-27).

While most pastors would like the tenacity of Moses or Paul, we grow weary from the steady stream of criticisms. Another church, another ministry, perhaps even another vocation becomes appealing at times. One of my pastor friends told me that his fantasy is win the grand prize of millions of dollars in some sweepstakes. He does not really desire to be wealthy; he simply wants to minister without answering to the critics in the church.

And while I will encourage all pastors and staff members to be tenacious in their ministries and churches in the midst of criticisms, I need to speak to laypersons as well. May I be blunt? How do you treat your pastor? Do you offer him words of encouragement? Do you pray for him? Are you willing to overlook his minor imperfections?

Or do you hold him to the CEO model of leadership? If he does not produce, is he out? Are you so nitpicky about everything he does that he is constantly looking over his shoulder, afraid to move lest he offend someone else?

Most of you laypersons are not divisive by nature. You are supportive of your pastor. But, possibly, when you hear the naysayers speak, you become quiet, lest you disrupt the unity of the church. Wrong! Your silence may be as deadly as the malignant and malicious words that are tossed about in the church.

Many pastors are indeed in pain. We thus have in many established churches the tension between the need for stability and long-term pastoral tenure, and the criticisms that drain the spirit of the pastor often prompt him to leave. How can church leaders remain effective in such an environment? Some lessons from the past may help.

A Model for Dealing with Criticism

Other than Jesus Himself, few Christian leaders personify the leadership skills necessary to deal with criticism as Abraham Lincoln did (see Donald T. Phillips, *Lincoln on Leadership* for a good treatment of this characteristic of Lincoln). Though he was not a pastor or staff member of a church, his response to the most malicious critics is a model for Christian leaders to this day.

Few people have been slandered, libeled, and hated during his leadership as much as Abraham Lincoln. He was the first Republican president, the result of a divided Democratic party. While Stephen A. Douglas and John C. Breckenridge were splitting votes by region, Lincoln won the election without even being on the ballot in most Southern states.

He was called every conceivable insult, including a third-rate country lawyer, a dictator, an ape, and a buffoon. One reporter described him as the craftiest and most dishonest politician in the history of America.

By the time he became president, Lincoln was the object of intense hatred from many different sides. Though many secular history books fail to mention his behavior as being like Christ's, it was a major reason he was able to lead a badly divided nation. Let's look at four key aspects of dealing with criticism in the life of Abraham Lincoln.

He Ignored the Attacks

Lincoln's frequent response to criticism was simply to ignore the most malicious attacks. The response was particularly true during election campaigns where the attacks were petty and ridiculous. Once he became president, he had to focus his energies on winning a war and holding a nation together.

The criticisms hurt Lincoln. Many of them came from people he believed to be friends of his. The pain was especially intense early in his political career. He became toughened to the critics later in life, but he never fully adjusted to the barbs thrown at him.

Yet Lincoln knew he could literally spend his entire career responding to attacks upon him. He had to decide, with God's wisdom, that much of the criticism could be ignored. In his last public address on April 11, 1865, he told the audience about his response to the innumerable criticisms: "As a general rule, I abstain from reading the reports of attacks upon myself, wishing not to be provoked by that to which I cannot properly offer an answer" (Phillips, 1992, p. 69).

He Occasionally Responded to the Critics

On occasion, however, Lincoln felt it was necessary to respond to some of the attacks. If a vital principle was at stake, if the office of the president was maligned, or if the unity of the nation was jeopardized, Lincoln responded. He could overlook petty barbs that hurt him only, but he would not tolerate the compromising of a principle or the unity of the nation.

During one of the Lincoln-Douglas debates, Stephen A. Douglas was applauded enthusiastically while Lincoln was jeered by the crowd. The central issue at stake was slavery. This time Lincoln stood up in public to the critics: "I am not going to be terrified by an excited populace, and hindered by from speaking my honest sentiments upon this infernal subject of human slavery" (Phillips, 1992, p. 69).

He Kept His Sense of Humor

Lincoln refused to let his critics take from him his joy for life and his keen sense of humor. His ability to laugh at himself and with others helped him to maintain a healthy perspective, while often disarming his critics. In response to several of Douglas' attacks on him in 1858, Lincoln told friends: "When a man hears himself somewhat misrepresented, it provokes him – at least, I find it so with myself; but when the misrepresentation becomes very gross and palpable, it is more apt to amuse him" (Phillips, 1992, p. 72).

He Did What Was Right – Regardless!

Abraham Lincoln truly believed that God was with him in his political career. He sought to please his Lord rather than others. As a result, he would enter into the decision-making process with confidence and assurance. Sure, the critics bothered him. He was a mere mortal. But ultimately he kept his focus on that which God led him to do.

Lincoln once said, "It often takes more courage to dare to do right than to fear to do wrong" (Phillips, 1992, p. 73). In a letter to General John McClernand the president wrote, "He who has the right needs not to fear" (Phillips, 1992, p. 73).

When Criticisms Come

Oliver Adderholt is the pastor of an established church. He has felt the sting of criticism for doing that which he honestly felt called by God to do. But the attacks have drained him emotionally, physically, and spiritually. He seeks the face of God. He needs the Father's wisdom to deal with the pain. God leads Oliver to handle criticism in the following ways.

The Power of Prayer

Pastor Adderholt rediscovers the abundant power of prayer, especially in dealing with criticism. He claims the promise of James 1:5 for God-given wisdom to handle all situations. He begins to pray specifically for his critics by name. His attitude toward them begins to change. To his surprise, many of his critics begin to change their attitude toward Oliver as well. Prayer opens the pastor's eyes. He learns not to be defensive as he had been previously. He also learns that he is not always right. The critics are sometimes right, at least partially so. Maybe they have the wrong intentions and wrong motivations, but sometimes they have a point.

Furthermore, prayer opens the eyes of Oliver to the real battle. His enemies are not critical church members, but invisible forces of Satan who have a singular purpose: to thwart God's work (Ephesians 6:12). The pastor realizes that when he yields to the distraction of the critics, when he loses his focus upon God's mission, then Satan has won a battle.

The Power of Love

From his prayer time Oliver began to sense the power of love. By praying for his critics he begins to love them. Those prayers were difficult at first, but he remains obedient to Jesus' mandate to love and pray for enemies (Matthew 5:44-45). His heart changes as he learns not only to love, but to forgive as well. The pastor realizes that he is a forgiven sinner just like his critics. The grace of God which was given to him is that same grace available to his enemies.

Learning to Ignore

Abraham Lincoln learned that he could not spend an entire political career responding to every criticism. Jesus Himself remained silent in the face of opposition more times than not. Oliver's ego was screaming for rebuttal and vindication in the midst of the attacks, but the pastor soon learned that silence was an effective tool. Today's crises and criticisms are quickly forgotten when the issues do not become an open debate.

Learning to Confide

Pastor Adderholt had spent so much time dwelling on the words of a few critics that he failed to realize that the great majority of the church had no idea what was taking place. He eventually found a few trusted leaders with whom he could share his frustrations. These men were leaders in the corporate and professional world who had taken their own share of criticisms. They knew how to empathize with Oliver, but they also helped him to keep his focus. "Don't let a few of these buzzards get you off track," Hank Wright responded in his usual blunt manner. Hank was the number two person in the largest bank in town, and he knew well the pettiness of critics. Such comments helped Oliver maintain a balanced perspective and not spend undue amounts of time worrying about detractors.

Respond on Occasion

There will be a few times in Oliver's ministry when a response will be necessary. The issue may be a central doctrinal truth, an ethical concern, or an issue that has the unity and testimony of the church at stake. The problem will be more than a personal complaint against the pastor.

Because Golden Road Church has seen their pastor handle criticisms with grace, and because they have seen his dependence upon God, they will be inclined to listen when he speaks. They know that Oliver has not blown up over every little problem that has come his way, so his speaking is an indication of the importance of the issue.

The response by the pastor may be painful to both him and the church but, on occasion, it is necessary. He cannot compromise principles and God's Word to avoid conflict. But God is with the pastor. And the Lord will see that good will come from this difficult situation because Oliver truly loves Him and seeks to obey Him (Romans 8:28).

Keeping Focused

Satan uses divisiveness to keep God's servants out of focus and off-kilter. The enemy knows that the energy pastors and their church leaders use to combat the critics is energy not available for sharing the gospel and doing God's work.

Oliver Adderholt has learned valuable lessons about criticisms. He never will enjoy them, but he has learned to deal with them. Above all, he is keeping his focus on leading the church toward that which God has called them to do.

By the way, the last time I spoke to Oliver, he was working on a sermon called "Staying Focused." His text was Philippians 3:13-14:

"Brothers, I do not consider myself yet to have taken hold of it. But one thing I do: Forgetting what is behind and straining toward what is ahead, I press on toward the goal to win the prize for which God has called me heavenward in Christ Jesus."

Keep pressing on, Oliver!

Growing through Criticism

Criticism is not always warranted, but all criticisms are opportunities to learn. When you are criticized, you can use it to grow or wilt as a leader. Most followers don't get excited about droopy leaders. Eeyore types don't often attract followers. Most churches don't want a pessimistic grey donkey full of sawdust in the pulpit.

What can you learn through criticism? Perhaps humility is the most difficult leadership trait to determine abo ourselves. And pride is the most dangerous leadership trait. Arrogance is the root leadership problems. Our sin nature propels us to an excessive and unhealthy focus on ourselves with we are criticized.

It's really the quintessential leadership struggle. We stand on a sliding scale somewhere between healthy humility and unhealthy pride.

Even at our best, determining where we are on this scale is tough. We almost always believe we are more humble than we really are. We rarely recognize our pride until it's too late. Fortunately, there are three key questions to ask to reduce the potential for pride to puff up as we are criticized.

Do you know your ministry, and are you striving to learn more? This question involves competence. Quite frankly, do you know what you're doing? Too many leaders fake it. Too many leaders do not want to swallow pride and ask for help. Too many leaders fear looking small by admitting they do not understand something. A lack of competence causes many leaders to guide an organization or church into unnecessarily risky waters.

Are you willing to sacrifice your career to do right thing? This question involves courage. Church leaders must be willing to make the hard and right decision no matter what the cost. Too many pastors make safe (but wrong) decisions because they fear personal repercussions from a vocal minority of critics. Integrity means making the tough decisions and taking the heat. Integrity also means verbally admitting fault when you're wrong.

Do you care about your followers as much as yourself? This question involves compassion. Do you love the people you're leading? If you don't, then why lead them? And why would they trust you? Don't leave unresolved conflict with your followers. Don't get offended every time a member corrects you. Don't be resistant to help from teams you manage. Be concerned about people on your leadership periphery—those that are on the outskirts of your leadership oversight. Do you know their names? Hob knob with quarterbacks and coaches—that's important—but never forget the name of the person carrying the water bottles.

The personal virtue of humility is a constant battle, but the most important one. Humility is a daily decision and a lifetime commitment. Leaders are doomed to short-term, arrogant decisions without competence, courage, and compassion. We can fool ourselves by losing focus on who we really are when we are criticized. When the aura of the position gets in the way of serving, we are no longer fit for the pastorate. Ultimately, we are merely pots. God is the Potter. He has ultimate control, not critics. And we should lead like we believe it.

The Problem of Personal Preferences

How many times has "I love you pastor, but..." ended with a request for someone's personal preference that has nothing to do with the vision and direction of the church. I'll never forget the church member who wanted to start a golf ministry. I was intrigued until he said it could only happen if the church bought an entire golf course.

Personal preferences—it's a topic that gets much water cooler talk within church leadership circles. Many pastors decry the elevation of churchgoers' preferences above God's mission. Rightly so. Anything that comes between God's people and God's mission is evil. It's why Jesus told Peter, "Get behind Me, Satan" (Matthew 16:23). Peter—with good intentions—was telling Jesus that suffering was not part of the Messiah's mission. But God's plan demanded a cross. Peter, however, preferred the kingdom come without a cross.

People in the church (many with good intentions) can demand silly things: music style, paint color, and programs. But what about pastors? Here's something with which I struggle as a pastor—I have personal preferences too. As a leader I can spin my *preferences* as *vision*. My position means I get the most opportunities to vocalize what I like. I am called to shepherd a congregation—leading them to join God's mission. But I can easily champion my preferences as the new direction of the church. So how do pastors detach their preferences from their vision? Let me share a few things I use as reminders that my "vision" is not necessarily what is best for the entire church.

True vision is shared. The best vision involves everyone. Great leaders find creative ways to get people on board. Vision is not the product of a lone ranger leader. Vision should be collective, encompassing the best from all members of the body. If I'm the only person who gets the vision, then I have failed in leading my congregation.

Intellect is not a weapon. If you use your intellect as a weapon, then you're not casting a vision. You're fighting for your preferences. Don't go around picking academic, historical, or theological fights with people that you feel need to acquiesce to your side. The purpose of theological training is not to get you ready for intellectual beat downs in the church.

Vision builds upon the past. Vision builds upon past successes, carrying the best of what was towards something greater. It never forgets the past, but helps propel people to places they did not think possible. If your vision does not include a celebration of past successes, then you're probably thinking too much about your own personal future preferences and opening up your leadership to criticism.

Growing as a Young Pastor

Allow me to use this space to address younger church leaders. While a pastor of any age can handle criticism poorly, younger church leaders tend to react more viscerally. Perhaps it is a lack of experience. Perhaps it is a lack of perspective that comes with age. Whatever the reason, young pastors often struggle with responding appropriately to critics. Though I'm approaching a decade as a pastor, I'm in my early thirties as I write these words. I'm guilty as anyone of hacking at the attackers.

Being a young(er) pastor, I've often heard from people who encourage me to "let no one despise your youth" (1 Timothy 4:12). These supporters are correct, and I'm thankful for their praise. As a pastor and leader, however, I often leave it there. I have thought to myself, "They're right. I'm not going to let anyone hold me back. I'll show them what I'm made of!" It's not the right reaction. It's not leadership to prove someone wrong in order to prop up a personal agenda.

As Paul writes Timothy he follows "let no one despise your youth" with leadership action items. "Instead," he articulates, "you should be an example to the believers in speech, in conduct, in love, in faith, in purity" (1 Timothy 4:12).

In other words, when people use your young age to bring you down, don't show them what you're made of. Don't set out to prove them wrong with success. It's a sophomoric response that proves them correct. The mature leader (regardless of age) will go out in front and show the way, leading by example. What does the example look like? Paul gives us guidelines:

In speech. The church places a higher standard on its leaders for what they say. While some people might get away with stray, snide remarks, you will not. Nor should you. Your congregation hangs on to your words more than other person in the church. Be careful how you are perceived. Snippy comments from leaders are magnified because of the position. When a senior pastor says something sarcastic or uncouth, it carries more weight. If you're young, it's magnified even more.

In conduct. You give up much privacy with a calling to lead a church, and you are always communicating through your actions. What events you attend (or don't) will get talked about. How much time you spend with certain groups or people will be discussed, and people will notice how you treat your spouse and children. Lead by setting the example in conduct.

In love. You must love your church where it is now. Your congregation will feel the distance if you only love them where you want them to be. Lead your church forward, but don't fall in love with the future while vilifying the present.

In faith. Do you really believe in your church? Whether people vocalize it or not, they will know if you do or don't. And if you don't believe in the people, then why are you there? Every church deserves a pastor who believes they can do great gospel work.

In purity. If your eyes lust through the computer screen, then you deserve the antagonism of a church that despises your youth. It's difficult to lead a church when you're grieving the Holy Spirit in your personal life.

Careful speech. Godly conduct. Real love. Genuine faith. And a pure heart. That's what true leaders are made of, whether they are praised or criticized.

----------- Chapter 4 ------------

Comfort

"We Can't Do That."

The two churches were located in different states, but the similarities between them were amazing. Both churches were in the same denomination. Both churches averaged about 200 in worship attendance. Both churches were located in communities of similar size with similar demographics. The two pastors of the churches were both in their early forties, and their perspectives were positive and visionary. Each church had recently completed a thorough evaluation of itself and its community. The demographics were favorable and the potential for both churches was excellent. On a mild autumn evening in October, each of the churches called meetings of the congregations to present the findings and to make recommendations for immediate action. Let us visit each of these meetings held seven hundred miles apart.

Newburg Church began its meeting promptly at 6:30 p.m. A sense of excitement filled the fellowship hall where the meeting was held. The chairman of the task force presented the findings of the group. With minimal remodeling and a new staff member responsible for small groups, the church could easily increase the attendance by 50 percent to 300 in two years.

The study first revealed the need for additional children's space. The preschool area, particularly, was near capacity. The growth in the church was coming from young families, and there was no reason why that would not be the case in the future. Future attendance increases were almost impossible because of space restrictions. But the thorough task force found that, with new room assignments and some remodeling, the new children's space could be created at a relatively modest cost.

The second recommendation addressed the need for a full time pastor responsible for small groups. While future growth would likely come largely from young families, small groups were key to retention of all members. The church already had a retired pastor working half time with small groups. He encouraged the church to delete his job and use his part-time salary to find a new full time small groups pastor. He would be happy to help the new staff member as a volunteer.

The response seemed surreal. One of the senior adult small group leaders, whose class had met in the same large room for 20 years, spoke next. "Well, I can't speak for all the ladies in my group, but it seems like we need to give our space to the preschool. Our average attendance is only six or seven, but 30 people could get in the room. Let us be the first to move. After all, this is Kingdom business!"

One of the "numbers" men in the church responded with equal enthusiasm. "I've done some calculating. With the funds from the current part-time positions, we only need to increase our attendance by 20 to pay for a full-time small groups pastor. I move we amend the budget and take that step of faith!"

Before the meeting concluded that evening, the proposal passed with a unanimous vote. The enthusiasm was contagious. The meeting concluded with everyone singing a praise chorus to the greatness of God.

Seven hundred miles to the south, however, Acacia Community Church members heard similar proposals. Their responses were vastly different than those at Newburg.

Mrs. Erskine spoke first: "If I'm hearing your recommendations correctly, my Sunday school class will have to move. I don't believe that is fair. We've been in the same Sunday school class for 20 years. Somebody else needs to move."

Then it was Mr. Flynt's turn: "Do you realize that our personnel costs will increase by seven percent with this one addition? And once you increase personnel expenses, it's almost impossible to decrease them. I'm firmly opposed to any staff additions."

Initially it sounded as if Mrs. Brown's words would change the direction of the meeting: "Now folks, it seems as if we have the opportunity to reach some people for Christ. We really need to find a way to do that. But we only have $6,000 in the bank. If only we had more money. . ."

The proponents of the proposal were stunned speechless. Before they knew what hit them, the motion had been tabled for "further study." But the naysayers had their way. The issue would never surface again.

Two years later the average attendance of Newburg Church had grown to 326. The attendance at Acacia Community Church was 163.

Two Churches, Two Responses

How could two churches of such similar circumstances and opportunities respond in such opposite fashion? Let's examine characteristics of both churches as they relate to their past and to their future.

The View of the Past

Newburg Church celebrated its past. The 30 year-old church consistently reminded itself that it was the fruition of the dreams and faith of a small number of visionaries. The past served as a reminder to move forward, to seek new and challenging ways to reach people for Christ. The past was the promise that God works miracles as His people are open to His will. They would never get comfortable, but would always be willing to take steps of faith.

Acacia Community Church remembered its 34 year-old past as well. Many of the members remembered the birth of the church and the construction of the new buildings. And a great number of the members longed to hold on to "the way we've always done things." Change was frightening to Acacia because it meant to them a departure from "the good old days" of the earlier years. Almost everything new was viewed as a threat because it was different from their church of the past.

The View of the Future

The members of Newburg Church are excited about the future. The days ahead present opportunities for ministry and growth. They have the faith that God will supply all their needs to reach their community. In essence the future will be better than the past or the present, because God's greatest blessings are yet to come.

The future frightens the naysayers at Acacia Community Church. They are worried about their personnel costs and their building costs. Their worry goes beyond prudence or fiscal responsibility; they really do not trust God to provide. The future is further a threat because it represents the potential to be different from the past. The past is security and comfort; the future is insecurity and discomfort.

The best days for the people of Newburg Church are viewed to be in the days to come. The best time for the people of Acacia Community Church have come and gone; they are in the past. Both churches will be proven correct in their perspectives.

The View of the Church Size

Newburg Church, primarily because it has a future mindset, sees itself as a large church. When the church had an average worship attendance of 200, the members realized that their church was larger than 75 percent of all churches in America. And when their attendance surpassed 300, they really felt like a large church.

The members of Newburg Church made plans with a larger-church mindset. They planned for future staff, more space, and larger budgets. They dreamed of new ministries and new outreach possibilities. They never thought they were too small to do God's will in their community. They were willing to get uncomfortable to do more in the future.

Acacia Community Church, on the other hand, saw itself as a small church with limited potential. As a result, most of the decisions made by the members of the church were to protect the status quo and to avoid further losses. They found comfort in the past. They tenaciously held on to their church ideal: their church of the late 1950s. Because of their perceived smallness, the church struggles for growth. The members become cliquish because new members are a threat to existing fellowship groups and the status quo.

A visionary pastor will become frustrated at a church like Acacia. If he seeks new members, the older members may feel threatened and neglected. Content with the status quo, they reject any new ideas or proposals.

Further, they may be controlling and possessive of the pastor and all that he does. Because they give their funds to the church, they often think they have a right to control the pastor. And many times the pastor grows weary and capitulates to the desires of the naysayers in the congregation.

The "We Can't" Obstacle

Acacia Community Church is the epitome of the "we can't" obstacle. It is almost unbelievable to visit and consult with churches that act as the God they serve is taking a nap for a few hundred years. The "we can't" obstacle manifests itself in several areas. Let me highlight a few.

Not Enough Money

Perhaps the most common stumbling block is the perception that the church just does not have the financial resources to do what they should be doing. Let me share a little "inside information" with church leaders, both lay leaders and staff. I have been in churches of all sizes, in every conceivable demographic situation, and with a wide range of growth rates. Guess what? All of the churches believe they need more money and larger budgets. Every one of them dreams of the possibilities in their church with greater financial resources.

The difference between the "can-do" churches and the "can't do" churches is how they respond to their present financial situation. "Can't do" churches will literally stop doing many ministries because they have money fears. They certainly would not consider any new ventures.

The "can-do" churches, on the other hand, will often go into new ministries without a clear indication of how the financial resources will be available for the venture. They do not act irresponsibly; they act on faith.

The attitude of the "can-do" church is that God does and will provide everything needed to do His will. They do not compare themselves with other churches and, in pity, bemoan their lack of resources. "Can-do" churches simply trust God for their finances. And God honors their faith.

The Problem with the Building

I spoke earlier of attitudes about church buildings. "Can't-do" churches like Acacia see limitations on growth because of the buildings. Not enough space. Not enough classrooms. Can't afford to add or to change the structure. Because of such attitudes, the building becomes the limitation to growth and the future of the church.

The difference between Newburg and Acacia was one of attitude. Newburg was able to raise a relatively small amount of funds to accomplish some needed renovations for space. Acacia could not see the possibility of raising funds, nor would they make the changes if the money was given to them.

Limitation of Ministries and Programs

Sometimes when I talk to leaders of smaller churches that are in close proximity to larger churches, an attitude of defeatism may be present. "We just can't compete with Eagle Run Community Church. They have so many programs and ministries. Why would anyone come to our church when they have so much to offer?"

Well, I have good news for smaller churches. Over one-half of those who attend church in America prefer a smaller church, less than two hundred in attendance. Instead of bemoaning their lack of programs and ministries, churches across our nation need to celebrate what God has given them.

The non-megachurches of America should view themselves as specialists that can do a few things well. That focus may be on a certain age group or a particular ministry. It probably will not be possible for your church to meet every need and every request. That is okay. That is why God gave us so many churches. Don't cry over what you do not have. Celebrate what God has given you. Reach and minister to many for Christ.

Staff Limitations

A fellow minister told me about a church where he had spoken. Almost one hundred single adults are in attendance on a given Sunday. While that number may seem impressive on its own, what is impressive is that the church has less than 300 in average attendance. What super staff person led the church in such outstanding outreach? Actually, there is no staff person of three full-time ministers who has responsibility for single adults. The ministry is led by a layman who feels called to single adult ministry, but also feels called to keep his job in the corporate world.

Too many churches take comfort in the staff doing the ministry. Once churches of all sizes get out of the mindset that a vocational minister has to initiate and maintain a ministry, then the supposed shortage of staff will not seem so critical. In fact, laypersons usually offer continuity and stability to ministry that the more mobile ministers can't always offer.

Yet there will be times that the staff additions will be necessary. The church will be faced with the choice of being a "can-do" Newburg Church or a "can't-do" Acacia Church. The church must maintain the balance of being financially prudent while taking the steps of faith to which God has called them.

Overcoming the "We-Can't Obstacle"

Thousands of established churches in every part of our nation are powerless and largely ineffective. They are comfortable with the status quo. Many of the members of these churches see earthly obstacles—lack of money, building limitations, inadequate staff, and others—but they cannot see the power of God that is sufficient to overcome any obstacles. How can pastors lead their churches toward a mindset that believes in God's possibilities? Let's examine five possible strategies.

Prayer... Again!

My constant mention of prayer throughout this book is not coincidental. Admittedly, many established churches are in dire straits. The church needs a miracle for a new attitude and an openness to God's work. It can happen! Ask God. I love the way the way the Holman Christian Standard Bible translates James 5:16: "The urgent request of a righteous person is very powerful in its effect."

Do you believe attitudes can be change with prayer? Do you believe that your prayers for your church can be powerful and effective? Take God at His word. There is no such thing as a helpless and hopeless church. It's time to pray.

Develop Allies

Pastors and other church leaders need allies who can pray with them, talk with them, and see God's possibilities for the church. Quite often the positive church members are intimidated by the actions of a few negative and recalcitrant individuals. As you develop allies, you will have a solid core group that will gain confidence to speak positively in both public and private settings.

It may even be advantageous to ask these allies to lead the discussion on important issues. Their words can set a positive tone and possibly silence the ever-present critics.

Focus on the Church's Strengths

Not even the largest churches can meet everyone's needs. God has placed unique persons with unique giftedness in churches of all sizes for a reason. He has also place your church in your community for specific reasons.

What are the strengths of your church? What aspect of your church's ministries can be celebrated and promoted? Help your members to focus on the ways that God is already working in your church. Take the spotlight off the ministries and programs you wish the church had. Make your present and potential ministries the focus of your celebration and praise. Count the blessings God has given you through your church, and let the community know about those blessings.

Challenge the People

A hunger is present in most Christians'

lives. A hunger to do something great for God, to be someone different for the Kingdom. Church members may act satisfied with the status quo; indeed they themselves may think they are content. But deep inside the heart of every Christian is a desire to break out of the shell of the common and to be a part of something miraculous.

The members of your church, especially those in staid and established churches, need to hear from you about God's power. They need to rediscover the power of the Holy Spirit who dwells within them. They need to hear sermons about Simon Peter, who walked on walked on water when he had his eyes on Jesus, but who sunk into the depths of the sea when he looked to the side and saw the difficulties and problems (Matthew 14:28-32). The members need to know that the normal Christian life is one of victories and even miracles. As one preacher said, "Christians must forever depart form the sameness, the lameness, and the tameness of life."

But you—pastor or staff member—you need to believe in the power of God yourself. Your life must be one of victories and faith. You cannot lead a people to a promised land unless you yourself have known the miracle of deliverance.

I have been in churches that are at death's door. I have also seen some of those churches become vibrant testimonies of God's work in their communities when the pundits said it could not be done.

Challenge your members. Reintroduce them to the God of miracles. Lead them to dream again. Lead them to open their eyes to God's possibilities. And remind them again and again of the words of the Savior whose strength is sufficient: "With men this is impossible, but with God all things are possible" (Matthew 19:26).

Solving Unsolvable Problems

What should you do if the culture of comfort has deep roots in your congregation? What if this attitude is a barrier to attaining the "ideal" solution? What if you got knocked down a few times in the first couple of rounds? Admittedly, some problems have staying power. And good leaders admit it when a solution to a problem will not come to fruition. Allow me to offer you two perspectives—one from the solution side and the other from the problem side. First, leaders can select the right problem to solve but craft a poor solution. Or they can attempt to solve the wrong problem.

Poor solution. Don't be guilty of wanting to hang on to your ideals—the best solutions—that you know are right, because sometimes the right solution becomes the wrong answer for a problem. Perhaps the solution was poorly communicated. Perhaps the solution was before its time. Perhaps you just didn't do a good job of selling it to the people. For whatever reason, the people being led just did accept it.

Wrong problem. Don't be guilty of trying to solve the wrong problems. You may be right. Those needing to change may be wrong. But sometimes leaders just pick the wrong battle. Don't be wrong for being right about the wrong problem.

As a pastor, I have been guilty of both—poor solutions to the right problems and good solutions to the wrong problems. I have fought needless battles. I have nitpicked problems. Clearly, sin problems in the church do not go unaddressed, and the Bible gives plain instructions on how to deal with sin. But some problems are not due to sin. They can be caused by poor planning, bad technology, odd traditions, and outside influences, among many others.

So what's a leader to do in these cases of unsolvable problems? What if you cannot ignore the issue? What if you must address the problem? These cases are not easy for leaders. Below are a few guidelines to consider.

Concede. Have self-awareness that your solution is not working. Acknowledge that you need a new plan. You "best" solution may never work (and it may really be the best solution). Sometimes leaders have to concede and settle for plan B. Sometimes followers will never grasp the best solution. Remember, leaders serve the people, not their own ideals.

Consensus. Most think of consensus positively—the majority opinion wins out. But the majority does not always have the right solution, nor do they always pick the right problems to solve. When consensus gets ugly, no one gets what they want but most can live with the outcome. Consensus can turn solutions sour and cause problems to perpetuate.

Leaders can use consensus, however, by building it. Don't start with a large bundle of ideas and allow the people to whittle down the options. Start with one or two new solutions and let the people build them up by making them their own.

Conversations. I've discovered something about leading the church—rumors work better if *you* start them. If you're shifting plans and proposing a new approach to an old problem, get feedback from the people through the rumor mill. Have low key conversations with key people and assume they will "talk." Then listen. Track the pulse of the body. Check the excitement (or dissatisfaction) level and continue crafting your solution.

Creativity. Conceding your ideal solution is not the same as admitting defeat. But it does require more creativity in building another solution. If the problem is unsolvable, then extra creativity is needed to find resolution. The problem may always be there. For instance, a landlocked, growing church in a downtown may not have the luxury of buying more land or building taller. Be creative in addressing the problem. If the problem is obvious, leaders can earn much respect by figuring out the next best solution.

When the Status Quo Works

This chapter is about breaking the status quo and making a church get uncomfortable to win a community. But not everything in the established church needs to change all at once. Indeed, no leader is capable of leading change in every area at the same time. Most churches need to change. Every church needs to change something. But not everything in every church needs to change. Sometimes the status quo works. How can you discern when to leave the status quo unchanged?

References to the status quo often evoke images of staleness, like weeks-old bread on your counter that is still technically edible but far from its original freshness. No one gets excited about crustiness, especially in the church.

There is a lot out there on changing, challenging, and deconstructing the status quo in churches. Rightly so—the status quo should not be used as a place of comfort or as a shield from potential criticism. And unfortunately, we have far too many examples of churches that are still technically working but far from their original freshness. You can smell their crustiness before you walk in the door.

The current sentiment is the status quo exists because people take comfort in it. Within the church culture, this desire for comfort is not healthy. But the status quo is just that—the prevailing state of affairs. These affairs may be good or bad, fresh or stale.

I admit much needs to change in many churches. However, not *everything* needs to change. Sometimes, "the way we've always done it" is a good thing. How do you know? What are some ways of looking at the prevailing state of affairs and discerning what to keep?

First, keep the status quo when it includes discipline. I run daily, out of habit. The discipline to run has become my status quo. When the discipline of ministry workers is the status quo, you will be a blessed ministry leader. If I were forced to bike daily, then the discipline to exercise might not stick. But the point is exercise to remain healthy, not necessarily what type of exercise you do. Be careful in changing the status quo in your church when the people are disciplined around a certain program. The point is the fruit of the program, not the program itself. If you're satisfied with the spiritual fruit, then be cautious in changing the program.

Second, keep the status quo when it includes passion. People often do the same thing over and over because they are passionate about it. When you kill the status quo, you often risk killing the passion of the church. You can work with passion. Passion killers often become targets. Pastors make for great targets. Don't hang one around your neck by unnecessarily squelching passion.

Third, keep the status quo when it is pragmatic. William James rattled the cage of the religious status quo with his philosophy of pragmatism in the early 1900s. He invented this philosophy for the common person, as something anyone could grasp. Ironically, the complexities of his philosophy didn't work for the commoner. I'm no supporter of James' philosophy as it applies to theology. However, church leaders can learn from what works in their churches. Pragmatism focuses on what works. If it is beneficial and helps accomplish a goal, then it is of value.

There's a reason you use air conditioning in the summer—it works to keep people in a comfortable climate to better the worship environment. Some things in the church just work well for the majority of people. Don't mess with them. Leading a church is not a science experiment where you can test creative causes and effects. If you turn off the A/C to see what will happen when you make people uncomfortable, your people will think you're mad. No one wants a mad scientist as a pastor. Sometimes it's best to stick with what works.

Why Average People Make an Excellent Church

I want to end this chapter on comfort by making a distinction between "average" and "comfortable." Let me make a bold claim: Average people are the best positioned congregants to help you break through the obstacle of comfort. Average is not the same as comfortable. Let me explain: I rarely encounter a normal church member. Now don't misread me. My church is full of everyday folks, but I don't often interact with them in their normal routines. Like most pastors, I see people more on the highs and lows. Nobody has ever called me and said, "Pastor, I ate oatmeal this morning. Nothing much happened at work. I came home, loved on my family, and watched evening news. I just thought you might want to know." Most people don't call when it's a normal day.

In reality, most of our churches are full of average people with normal lives. Church members, please don't miss God's grace in the normality of your routine. Normal days of emails, vacuuming, and PB&Js are amazing blessings. Pastors, don't let seeing the best and worst of people in their extremes cloud your judgment about who they really are. And please don't assume people are comfortable just because they have a regular routine. They may just be disciplined.

In all reality, most people in the church just want to raise godly kids, remain faithful, help out their friends and neighbors, and share Christ in their local community. Without a doubt, the creative types in our churches add some much needed flavor. However, the majority of our congregations are not obsessed with the latest trends in fashion, music, and technology. And on any given day, almost everyone—normal or not—hopes to put their kids to bed without an epic meltdown spilling into the morrow.

I believe my congregation would describe "normal" as faithfulness to a local body, faithfulness to a family, and faithfulness to Christ. I like that kind of normal. But I also want my church to be willing to get uncomfortable for the sake of the gospel. Average people make for an excellent church because they are likely to resonate with the largest group in your community on a personal level. The very definition of average points to what is typical. So bring on more Camry-driving people. Why? Because the church needs them to win the masses for Jesus.

Chapter 5

Expectations

"Why Didn't You Visit Me?"

Meet Carl. Carl is the pastor of West Cove Congregational Church in a college town in Texas. Like many pastors, Carl does not really have a typical day, but we will follow him around on this particular Tuesday. We will see if his day has any unusual twists to it.

West Cove is a typical established Texas church. Average worship attendance is 180, and the church has experienced modest growth in Carl's four-year tenure.

The pastor has experienced highs and lows in his time at West Cove, but there are no major problems in the church of which he is aware.

The alarm awakens our friend rudely at 5:30 a.m. Carl spends 30 minutes in prayer and devotional Bible study. For the next hour after that, he helps his wife get their three children ready for school. Then he shaves, showers, and heads to the church by 8:15 a.m. He greets his assistant and begins preparation for one of his sermons.

Thirty minutes into his sermon preparation, his assistant knocks on the door. Betsy Franks has been taken to the hospital with chest pains. Carl marks his place in his Bible and takes the 15-minute drive to the hospital. He stays with Betsy and her family until the danger has passed and heads back to the church. He arrives at 11:30 a.m. and decides to skip lunch. He really needs to study.

At 1:00 p.m. his assistant reminds him of the committee meeting at the local church association. "Can't I get out of it?" he complains. She knows the question is rhetorical, but she responds anyway: "No way." Carl is the committee chairman.

Finally at 3:00 p.m. he settles back into his office, ready to resume his sermon preparation. His assistant sticks her head in the door. "Your 3:00 p.m. appointment is here," she informs him. *What appointment?* he wonders. His smartphone calendar answers his question. The Michaels are coming in for counseling. Their marriage is shaky. Carl meets with them until 4:30 p.m.

A heavy inbox of emails await the pastor after the counseling session. He decides to tackle the emails for an hour. That will give 30 minutes to return a few calls, 30 minutes for dinner with his family, and then on to his 6:30 p.m. appointment with the Wilders. They are a young couple who want to talk about becoming members of the church.

The first call he returns is Mrs. Ikerd. Carl knew she had called earlier in the afternoon, but he just couldn't get to it. He jokingly thought to himself that the message just might disappear. He takes a deep breath, dials the number, and waits. "Hello, Gladys, this is the pastor returning your call." The other voice responds: "It's about time! I called you four hours and 12 minutes ago!"

Carl bites his lip and says calmly, "What can I do for you Gladys?" The church member responds with sanctimonious indignation: "Pastor, people are talking. They don't believe you are spending enough time in the office, and there have been tons of complaints about the fact that you don't visit enough. I bet you didn't even care that I was sick with the flu all last week. Why didn't you visit me?"

The "Carls" of This World

Every pastor can identify with Carl regardless of the size of the church. Pastors are in a vocation that is the epitome of paradox. On the one hand, the job has no direct supervision. He has the freedom to be a total goof-off or a hopeless workaholic. Most pastors lean toward the latter.

On the other hand, a pastor reports to everyone, regardless of church polity. At least most members think so. Each church member is his boss. Many members think that, because they pay his salary, they have every right to keep him in line.

Several years ago, when my dad was a pastor, he gave a survey to the 12 deacons in his church. He listed several congregational responsibilities and asked them to share the *minimum amount of time* he should average in each area each week. He listed about 20 areas; but they were free to add on blank lines.

In order to meet the *minimum expectations* of the deacons, he had to fulfill the following responsibilities each week:

Prayer at the church: 14 hours
Sermon preparation: 18 hours

Outreach and evangelism: 10 hours
Counseling: 10 hours
Hospital and home visits: 15 hours
Administrative functions: 18 hours
Community involvement: 5 hours
Denominational involvement: 5 hours
Church meetings: 5 hours
Worship services/preaching: 4 hours
Other: 10 hours

Total: 114 hours/week

If he met just the minimum expectations of 12 deacons, he would have to work over 16 hours a day for seven days a week. Or he could take one day off work each week, and work 19 hours a day for six days a week. And remember, he still would only meet the minimum expectations of 12 people in the church, not the entire membership.

Clearly a pastor will sense the tension of so many factors competing for his time. How he handles that tension may very well determine if will be successful in his leadership of the established church.

Handling the Time Pressures

Several years ago, Chuck Swindoll would write and preach about the "tyranny of the urgent." He was specifically referring to Christians who spend their lives going from one urgent event to the next. Simple lives with ample time for prayer, Bible study, family, and friends are little more than dreams for most.

Pastors and other church leaders experience the tyranny of the urgent as much as any group of which I am aware. Some people may have the idealistic view of pastors' lives. They might envy a life that they think is spent mostly in hours of prayer and study of the Bible. Oh, they might have an occasional wedding, funeral, or hospital visit, and they would have to prepare sermons. But, for the most part, a pastor's time was hours of spiritual retreat. Wrong!

A leader in an established church will feel considerable tension in where he spends his time. On the one hand, established church pastors are often expected to be directly involved in time-consuming one-on-one ministry. On the other hand, such ministry takes away from sermon preparation, strategic planning, and other macro ministries.

Many pastoral leadership books of recent years indicate an inverse relationship between pastors who minister personally with people and the growth potential of the church. I would agree that prospects for greater growth are not as good for the pastor who *literally wears himself out* meeting the needs of every church member. Yet it is dangerous to carry that principle to the opposite extreme. *A pastor of an established church who does little or no personal ministry is setting himself up for major problems in the future.*

Such is the tension that must be managed by the pastor: time spent in strategic endeavors and time spent in personal ministries one-on-one. The pastor of the established church who spends most of his time in strategic ministries will soon hear the complaints: "He doesn't have time for us. He cares more about growing a church than ministering to members. He's not a very warm person."

Established church pastors will not solve the problem of this tension. They must learn to deal with it and live with it. Balance and wise time management are keys to living with this tension.

Perhaps a few tips of basic time management will prove helpful here.

Keep Track of Your Time

The late Peter Drucker advocated that one of the most distinguishing factors between an effective executive and an ineffective executive was how he or she took care of time. Many of those same principles can be applied to established church pastors.

Do you know how every minute of your day is spent? Have you ever kept a time log for two or three days? Did you know that you can change your behavior just by recording your time? Are you spending adequate time in those areas that are most important to you and God? Try the time log experiment for a couple of days. Watch every minute. It's usually incredibly revealing.

Become a Better Steward of Time

In a number of consultations, my team has seen one particular area that consumes large chunks of a pastor's time: visiting people who are in the hospital. Pastors in small towns and rural areas often must travel to other cities to visit the hospitalized church members. City and suburban pastors often find themselves going from one section of the city to another to different hospitals.

In this area of ministry particularly, church leaders need to plan their day carefully. Except for emergencies or life-or-death situations, a few minutes with each hospitalized church member is adequate. In fact, a sick person usually welcomes a brief visit.

I've looked at lists from church consultants on the most common time wasters for ministers. See if you can identify with any of these: nonproductive time on the Internet; too much time dealing with emails; self-imposed interruptions (such as studying and finding something else interesting on your desk); failure to use voice mail on your smart phone; opening useless mail; over-preparation; handling mail and other papers multiple times; unstructured visits; spending too long visiting; poor reading habits; sleeping in; procrastination. Can you make improvements in any of these areas?

Establish Priorities

If the "tyranny of the urgent" is one problem for ministers, then the "captivity of the mundane" is another. How many hours do we spend each week on tasks that are relatively unimportant?

Have you ever made a true priority list? Write down those things that need to be done, in order of importance. But here's the key. Don't start any item on the list until you have completed the one before it. Repeat that exercise every day, even if you have carryover tasks.

One of the reasons we never seem to get anything done is that we move from one task to another without finishing our highest priority items.

Become Organized

Do you find yourself going from one task to another with virtually no system or organization? Learn to group your activities. Set aside *on your calendar* one hour to answer emails. Set aside *on your calendar* an entire half-day for sermon preparation. If you have an assistant, let him or her know that sermon preparation is on the calendar just like a counseling appointment. It can't be interrupted except for emergencies.

Some time management experts recommend that we divide our workweek into 42 four-hour segments. We can thus plan each day by six different activities: family time and sleep; church work and study time, and so on. We do not become easily frustrated with minute-to-minute interruptions because we work in four-hour segments.

Technology has given us a plethora of time management tools with smart phones and apps. Do some searching to see what can help you the most. Ask a fellow pastor who seems to be efficient with his time what technology tools he uses.

It's Okay to Say "No"

You will never have enough time for anything until you learn the magic of the little word "no." You cannot do everything. You have responsibilities to God for prayer and Bible study. You have responsibilities to your family. You have primary responsibilities to your church to preach, shepherd, and equip. You have responsibilities to yourself for rest and leisure activities.

Do you realize that, in the long term, you are actually hurting your church by saying "yes" to all their requests? The members of your church need to learn that they do not need you for every meeting, social activity, or ministry. Perhaps it will take a while to instill that mindset. As you sever the bond of pastoral dependency and equip your members for doing ministry, your church will become healthier and more productive for the glory of God.

The Power of Delegation

Not only can you say "no," you should also empower others to do ministry and activities. One of the most frequent lines that church members bring to pastors is "Pastor, our church needs. . ." You can respond: "That's great. God has obviously given you this burden. You are now chairperson of an ad hoc group to see what it would take to get this done, and to make recommendations to us. Let me know what you find."

Learn to delegate! Make equipping the saints to be one of your highest ministry priorities.

You may think that no one can do it better than yourself, but you will do nothing well if your try to do it all.

When Spiritual Gifts Are Discovered

I find myself returning to 1 Corinthians 12-14 again and again in my ministry. This passage, and the spiritual gifts passages in Ephesians 4:11-13 and Romans 12:6-8 are critical in our understanding of the proper stewardship of our time resources.

The result of a church functioning according to spiritual gifts is a church where the work of ministry is distributed to every member. No church member, including the pastor, has an excessive burden. Church members are not a part of the body of Christ to be spectators. They are to be functioning in the life and work of the church to do the work of ministry. And, because they are doing ministry according to their giftedness, work at the church is a joy and not a burden.

Spiritual gifts discovery and utilization has two primary benefits related to time stewardship. It frees the pastor to do his ministry according to his giftedness and passions. And it empowers the members of the church to be in ministry that might otherwise fall into the overloaded hands of "hired help."

Spiritual Gifts Discovery by the Pastor

I am amazed at how few church leaders today really know their own spiritual gifts. Meeting the needs of others will never be effective until we leaders fully understand ourselves and the ways God has wired us.

For example, one pastor shared with me that he really did not like counseling. In fact, he dreaded the counseling appointments he had each week. He was given the opportunity to do a spiritual gifts and personality assessment. He found that his spiritual gift mix was not conducive at all for a counseling ministry. He was, however, gifted in administration or leadership.

This awareness helped him to see how his ministry had struggles. First, he realized that he had a tendency to place counseling responsibilities on the back burner since his gifts and desires were not in this area. But he also realized that as a pastor he could not relinquish all counseling responsibilities to others. He began to make special efforts to be available and open for those who really wanted to share their burdens with him. He did not want to give them the impression that he did not care for them, or that he didn't want to see them.

Second, he was honest with the church members that counseling was not his strength. He would always have an open door for them but, in the long run, others could help them more than he could. And that reality brings me to his final step.

Third, he would delegate counseling responsibilities when possible. Two laypersons were trained and equipped to handle a large portion of the counseling load of the church. A staff minister with a spiritual gift mix conducive to counseling began handling much of the ministry as well. Finally, some members were referred to Christian counselors in the area. They had the professional training and experience the others did not have.

The point is simple. The pastor knew his spiritual gifts. He knew where he was not gifted. So he made plans to strengthen his strengths and compensate for his weaknesses. As a result, he made much more efficient use of his time, and he made more significant contributions to the church through his ministry. From a time stewardship perspective, the more people are involved in ministry, the more time a church leader will have to do the tasks God has called him to do.

The Roots of Unrealistic Expectations

How and why do unrealistic expectations begin in the first place? What are some ways church leaders feed this mentality? There is a romance of leadership. I'm not referring to romantic feelings, but rather an imbalanced fascination many people have with pastors. Our churches can glamorize the shepherd role, which is, quite frankly, terribly ironic.

Most scholarly studies in leadership focus on the top roles. Many leader-centric approaches assume followers are mere recipients of leader-driven change. To romance leadership is to exaggerate its importance relative to followers. Leadership is extremely important, but it exists only because followers collectively interpret someone (or a group) in such a role. Romancing leadership leaves out half the relationship. Followers are just as important. Obsessing over leaders at the expense of followers leaves a gaping hole in understanding how leadership really works. And it creates a system where people in the church have unrealistic expectations of pastors and other church leaders.

In 1978 James MacGregor Burns published his seminal book, *Leadership.* This work shifted and shaped the paradigm on leadership studies. As a result of his work, researchers and biographers discussed less the character traits of leaders and focused more on the engagement of leaders with their followers for a common goal. Burns' book focused primarily on the political sphere, but his leadership theories struck a chord with many, including the church. The main idea that Burns proposed was a differentiation between transactional and transformational leaders.

Transactional leaders utilize a social exchange to accomplish their goals. The example of politics is used frequently: "You vote for me and I'll do this for you." These leaders use a quid pro quo to lead. In the financial world, this exchange can take the form of incentives for productivity or disincentives for a lack of productivity. Those with the authority are able to offer something in exchange for a following. And they can take away things when followers don't follow well. In the church, pastors can react transactionally with members. Members give, supporting the salary of the pastor. The pastor then feels the obligation to minister.

Transformational leaders operate much differently. These leaders inspire people to reach for a common goal. They develop, train, and mentor future talent. They empower people to accomplish tasks. Creativity, transparency, and authenticity are valued. Leaders and followers alike know what the goal is and how to achieve it. These leaders show everyone the big picture and why it's important. In this type of environment, the pastor no longer *responds* to unrealistic expectations but rather *sets* the proper expectations. The church and pastor then equip people together to accomplish a common goal.

For the most part, church leaders should act in a more transformational capacity. There are times for transactional leadership. A sergeant under fire in a foxhole needs to use his authority without explaining the "big picture" to everyone. Sometimes pastors really do need to react to a crisis. In general, however, the idea is to motivate people with a common purpose and not press them in a certain direction with power-wielding authority.

Unfortunately, I see too much transactional leadership in the established church. It can take a couple of forms: autocratic pastors or power-hungry parishioners letting everyone know who pays the bills. Clearly, these two examples are polar extremes, but they do emerge in lesser degrees. The greater problem that occurs in many churches is the level of comfort derived from a transactional environment. A group of people give to the church; the pastor mollycoddles them. Faithful stewardship and caring for a flock are biblical, but an exchange for the two is not healthy.

Why Churches Keep Bad Pastors

All of the blame for unrealistic expectations does not fall on the people of the church. Some pastors are not good leaders. Have you ever wondered why some churches hang on to a leader who is obviously toxic? If followers have power and influence, then why might they fall prey to unreasonable expectations from the church leader? How can the leader-follower relationship break down? What makes followers susceptible to toxic leadership? Followers and leaders share the blame. Bad pastors and willing congregants create this environment together.

Safety. In most situations, unfollowing a leader is almost as simple as the aptly named Twitter button. Most people are not locked into a leader. You can leave a church. You can transition out of a job. You can transfer schools. People can vote out politicians and strike against companies. Most followers in our culture have the freedom to walk away. But with every increase in freedom comes a corresponding decrease in safety. If you walk away from your job, then the paycheck is no longer guaranteed. If you vote out a politician, then you risk voting in one who is worse. In short, followers stick with bad leaders because they are not willing to risk safety in order to be free.

Belonging. Ditching a bad leader may mean leaving an important community. For instance, many followers remain loyal to a professional sports team despite an unscrupulous owner or ineffective coach. Loyalty is a powerful force within a community. Belonging in a human community will often supersede leaving a group leader. It's why some churchgoers tolerate a fruitless pastor. It's why cult followers do not denounce the cult after the leader falters catastrophically. Unfollowing a toxic leader is often more painful (and less important) than the sense of belonging that comes from the community over which the leader presides.

Comfort. Challenging bad leaders is uncomfortable (at best) and deadly (at worst), but many followers forget they have the power to challenge leaders. In fact, dual accountability is one of the keys to a successful leader-follower relationship. In order to challenge leaders, however, followers must let go of comfortable silence. If you are the only one to speak out, and no one joins you, then you're left alone in a vulnerable and uncomfortable position. Many followers are not willing to risk comfort to challenge bad leaders.

A healthy leader-follower relationship is less about an exaggerated leader romance and more about dual accountability. Accountability is what prevents leaders from becoming dictators and tyrants. Church members need pastors to help guide them to better places. Pastors need church members in order to fulfill their purpose and calling. And both pastors and church members should rely totally on the providence of God, not safety, belonging, and comfort.

The Proper Tone of Pastoral Leadership

One of the best ways to set reasonable expectations in the church is to use the proper tone with communicating with your congregation. Finding the voice in which to communicate content is sometimes just as difficult as determining the content itself. In other words, *how* you communicate is an important component of *what* you communicate. Content is critical, but so is delivery.

As a senior pastor, I set the tone of the church. My heart in writing such a statement is not arrogance but rather self-awareness. Of any leader in the church, I know my vision—and how I communicate it—will affect the church more than any other person. Even though I believe vision is a collective effort of leaders and followers, the communicator of the vision has a special prominence. Since I am often the first to communicate the content of the vision, my delivery of the content will affect the tone of how the church receives it. Therefore, finding my voice as a leader is critical to the actual vision of my church.

How might leaders set the tone in their organizations? What different voices might they use in communicating vision? I've listed a few different options for church leaders.

Coach. Use a coach's voice if you want to get people pumped up about something. This voice works well when you are relaying positive news while attempting to recruit people to serve. An in-your-face-yet-encouraging coach will set the tone of enlistment with excitement.

Theologian. Not all theologians are leaders, but all leaders within the church should be theologians. Not every church situation, however, requires a leader to communicate as a theologian. A pastor should use this voice when working through difficult biblical issues. How will the church handle the problem of divorce? What is the church going to do about a multiplicity of viewpoints among the congregation on a particular topic? A theological voice helps set the tone of looking at the issue with the proper amount of emotion.

Engineer. Inevitably, most churches will have a group of people who attempt to solve problems from a structural perspective. For them, problems are solved with policies, Visio charts, and spreadsheets. While not all vision needs to be structural in nature, vision does require structure for proper implementation. Church leaders and pastors should use the voice of an engineer when communicating this structure, especially to the group of people who default to the structural frame.

General. Few want to be on the receiving end of a general barking orders on a regular basis. When a crisis hits, however, someone must step up quickly and take charge. When a vision includes a real sense of urgency, the voice of a general becomes an effective way to set the tone of urgency among followers.

Friend. Some leadership visions require less of an inspiring appeal to the masses and more of a friendly interaction with followers. Using the voice of a friend sets the tone of long term buy-in and loyalty among followers.

Leaders should use different voices in different venues with different groups of people in order to set the proper tone within a church. Followers will respond to the tone of leadership just as much as the actual content of the vision. Match the correct tone with the right content and people in the church will begin to have more reasonable expectations.

"So. . . Why Didn't You Visit Me?"

We met Carl, the pastor of West Cover Congregational Church, at the beginning of this chapter. He had encountered the ever-so-common obstacles in an established church of time constraints and ministry expectations.

Will the principles stated in this chapter solve all of Carl's ministry demands? No. The tension will be present. The expectations of an established church pastor are high, but you can see the situation improve. The pastor can find more time available for vital ministries.

And lest you forget, the implementation of every principle stated in this chapter and this book will take time. Leading an established your church over obstacles like insufficient time and unrealistic expectations may take a few years. But it can be done. Wait on the rewards.

------------ Chapter 6 ------------

Putting It All Together

The Healthy Established Church and Her Pastor

My wife and I went on a cruise for our honeymoon. On the boat I had my devotional time on our balcony, overlooking the sea. The smell of salt water and the feel of a warm breeze made for great January weather. The sea appears endless from a cruise ship, reaching as far as the sky and ultimately ending on the horizon. As I finished my prayer time, I could only imagine the way in which earlier sea-farers traveled. I had the creature comforts of a king-sized bed, private bathroom, running water, and the largest cornucopia of food you have ever seen (and ice-sculptures to boot). But the Spanish explorers, the Puritans, and the Apostle Paul all faced a much harsher trip when crossing the seas.

I imagined Peter at Simon the tanner's house in Joppa, looking out into the sea and seeing the ends of the earth, realizing that God has called him to a global mission, not knowing what would happen or how he would reach where the sky meets the sea. He had plenty of daunting obstacles: Geography, culture, and language.

Seeing the vast expanse that was before me, I realized that I too am called on the same global mission, that as a pastor I am to preach the gospel message to all who would hear and to send those willing to go to the far corners of the earth. All of us who claim the name of Jesus Christ are called. The Great Commission is not optional. You *will be* Christ's witnesses as the imperative states in Acts 1:8.

Then I began to think about all the times that I had failed this mission, how many times God had placed before me someone who needed to hear about Christ's amazing grace, and I had remained silent. Just that previous night I had not been obedient. There was a man on the cruise at our table who stated, "It's all about being a good person" when I asked him about his church and faith. I could have used his response as a prompt into the gospel, but I rationalized that it wasn't the right timing.

But it's not about our timing; rather it is God's timing. And when God places people in our lives, our love for Christ should spill over, so much so that we can't stop speaking about Jesus Christ, no matter what the circumstance.

We are all on a mission. We as Christians are all in the same boat. Whether God calls us to the far corners of the earth or our own backyards, our passion for the gospel should be unceasing. The good news is that our mission doesn't end when we aren't as obedient as we should be. God doesn't cut us off after one failure. There could be as many as 250 million people in the United States that don't know Christ. Globally, the number reaches into the billions. There are people in every walk of life that need Jesus.

Churches should weep over these souls. We should pray earnestly for softened hearts and for opportunities to tell the gospel message. And we should be willing to go to where the sky meets the sea in order to share the only Truth that can save a soul.

Leading an established church is not always easy, but it can be immensely rewarding. And we need dedicated and gifted leaders in these churches. Depending on how you count and define the churches, there are as many as 300,000 of them in the United States alone.

As you lead an established church to greater health, you will have to demonstrate a great deal of balance. Being an established church pastor is an exercise in paradox. Look at a few of the tensions you must keep in balance.

Spiritual and Pragmatic

You must give priority to prayer. You must be open to new methodologies that will help your church become healthier. You will need to be a consumer of the latest practical writings on church health, but you must also be aware that only a sovereign God can send real revival. You must depend totally on God, but not take lightly the counsel of godly men and women. You must ask: "What works?" but you must realize that tools are only for a season.

Tenacious and Flexible

Because you are the pastor of an established church, longer tenure is very important. Unless God clearly calls you to another ministry, you will need to be tenacious about your calling, even in the most difficult of times. Satan would love to see you so discouraged that you are ready to give up.

Yet while you must be unswerving in your commitment to your church, you must demonstrate an abundance of flexibility in dealing with your members. The roles that you will be asked to fill may change ten times in one day. At the end of the day, you may not know if you are coming or going!

Action-Oriented and Patient

Established churches need pastors who take initiative and lead the people to new challenges. The churches must be shaken from their complacency to see the possibilities of God. But established churches also need pastor who have patience, who can wait on God's timing without much frustration, especially when it seems that nothing is happening. Established churches need pastors who have the wisdom to know when to move or when to wait.

Sensitive and Tough-Skinned

Pastors, don't you love it when you have

just been through a round of criticisms and a well-meaning church member tells you to get your act together? "Pastor, you just have to have tough skin. You can't let everything hurt you."

Yet before the week is over, you may be taken to task for your insensitivity for not visiting someone. That particular church member may even articulate that you are just not sensitive enough.

Such is the tension that is, and will continue to be, a part of your life. Certain occasions will call for you to have the hide of a rhino, while others will demand you be sensitive and caring. How do you reconcile the two demands on your life? You don't. You recognize that God will provide for all your needs for each and every occasion (Philippians 4:19).

Ambitious and Content

You must have a desire to see your church grow, to reach people for Christ, to reach new heights. You need to set ambitious goals and challenge your members to meet them. You must believe that the God you serve is a God of miracles, and that He will work miracles in your church.

You must be content with what may seem to be like the pace of snail. And you can't be discouraged because your church is not like the larger and more active church in the community. You must be ambitious, yet you must be content. It is a paradox. But you're in good company. The Apostle Paul dealt successfully with that same paradox. If you are doubtful, read both Philippians 3:14 and 4:12. He did it. So can you.

Traditional and Contemporary

You must lead your church to reach a contemporary world. Some of the methods must change if that possibility is to ever become a reality. But you must be willing and even eager to hold on to some of those traditions that really matter.

Your church is to "become all things to all people," so that by all means some might be saved (1 Corinthians 9:22). But your church must not conform to the pattern of the world (Romans 12:2). You must lead your church to be in the world but not of the world.

Management and Leadership

A dialogue continues among researchers about the differences between managers and leaders. It is clear that there is overlap between the two roles. It is equally clear that some managers do not lead, and some leaders do not manage. A helpful (but ultimately inadequate) distinction is that managers deal with maintaining consistency in the here and now, while leaders work to change the future.

Pastors of congregations hold both roles (among many others). They lead. They manage. There is an overabundance of material that addresses the pastor as leader. Less research has been done about the pastor as manager. The managerial side of pastoring can be frantic on any given day. The pace can switch from comfortable to chaotic with one phone call. Most people understand and respect this aspect of ministry. What is less known is how fragmented daily activities are. Much pastoral management can occur in short conversations and activities: 10 minutes here, 15 minutes there. Quick, hopscotch exchanges are normative in daily management of the church.

The management role of a pastor surfaces in many different functions. You are a liaison. Pastors are the spokespeople and representatives for their churches in the community. They should work to make new contacts, connect with other leaders, and communicate a positive message on behalf of the congregation.

You are a mediator. While pastors should not be expected to handle every conflict within the church, they do handle sudden crises. Pastors that are good managers step in at appropriate times when disturbances occur between members or with outside people.

You are a juggler. Pastors are expected to lead many teams comprising of laity and staff. Planning appropriately requires pastors to juggle several meetings and exchanges with different people.

You are an observer. Pastors should monitor the health of the church. They track the pulse of the congregation. Part of this observer role requires weekly knowledge of relevant church metrics. How is involvement in small groups trending? How is the worship service attendance tracking? What are ministry teams doing?

You are a disseminator. Since pastors touch base with many different groups and segments of the church (probably more so than any other person), they are in the unique position of knowledge gatekeeper. Part of managing a congregation requires pastors to disseminate information acquired from one group to another group. They help connect people and tasks for more efficient ministry.

Encouragement, Hope, and Promise in the Trenches

The local church is the front line of ministry. In the battle against the spiritual forces of evil, the church is the trench. Christ's bride is dug in, charged up, and ready to die for the freedom of souls. I relish the trench. It's messy, at times gruesome, and the noise makes it difficult to sleep. But I love it.

While there is no beauty in warfare (spiritual or otherwise), the battling bride is a gorgeous organism. Despite the muck, despite the damage, and despite the fight, she remains pure, white, and righteous. She belongs to Christ. She combats for Christ. She never stops engaging in the mission of reclaiming captives of darkness. The fighting white bride shines in the gray of spiritual war.

As a pastor, I realize the gravity of decisions I make. Vision isn't just a compelling statement of future growth. Programs aren't just tools for assimilating more people. Church events are far more than ways to make the community come to the campus.

When you invite someone to church, you're calling them down into the trench. When you talk to someone about joining the mission, you're asking them to suit up and grab a gospel grenade. The church is currently fighting a battle which will lead to ultimate victory. We win. Satan loses. And Jesus reigns. But we still must fight. The beautiful bride is a battling warrior.

Let's stop pretending our churches are polished platforms of sanitized morality, speaking sentimentality apart from Truth. Let's burn the preferences of wooden traditionalism. Let's quit the silly game of worship experience one-upmanship. Let's elevate spiritual grit above smooth and seamless operations. We're in the middle of a serious war. Let's get real about what we believe and who we're really following. When

King Jesus returns, will he find the faithful in the trenches or in comfortable country clubs?

So we dig in. War is not won when soldiers retreat. Victory does not come to indifferent combatants. I've been guilty of placing myself on a pedestal. I've tried to climb into the ivory tower. I've ridden a few high horses. And I've found I'm at my best when I'm covered in mud in the trench of the local church. I'm fighting most fiercely when I'm not worried about my personal brand. I'm fighting well when I'm more concerned about the local pregnancy clinic than who retweets one of my pithy—but ultimately useless—140-character oddments.

Your role as the leader of an established church is not an easy one. Indeed it is an impossible role without the strength of the Lord. I am in contact with many established church pastors and staff members across the nation. I am one myself. I would never minimize the conflict, struggles, and pain that I see in many of these churches.

But something is happening. A fresh wind is blowing. It might not be in many churches yet, but something is happening. Churches once declared comatose or terminal are now seeing new life. The

Holy Spirit is giving a new beginning to churches that once seemed hopeless.

I wrote this book as a book of hope for a new generation of pastors. I have prayed that these words would reach pastors, staff persons, and laypersons who most needed to hear words of hope and encouragement.

You have been called. You are as certain of your call as your salvation. My friend, God has not called you to a ministry of futility; He has called you to a ministry of fulfillment.

The established church is a challenge. But you have been called to serve and love people in these churches. You will not only meet the challenge, but you are yet to see the most fruitful days of your ministry. My promise? No, God's promise: "I am sure of this, that He who started a good work in you will carry it on to completion until the day of Christ Jesus" (Philippians 1:6).

Carry on. Be encouraged. Stand faithful. The best days of your ministry are about to begin. Dig in and fight.

Made in the USA
Lexington, KY
25 November 2014